A Safe Future

Reducing the
Human Cost
of War

Edmund Cairns

Oxfam
Publications

Available from the following agents:
for Canada and the USA: Humanities Press International, 165 First Avenue, Atlantic Highlands, New Jersey NJ 07716-1289, USA; tel. (908) 8721441; fax (908) 8720717
for Southern Africa: David Philip Publishers, PO Box 23408, Claremont, Cape Town 7735, South Africa; tel. (021) 644136; fax (021) 643358
for Australia: Bush Books, PO Box 1370, Gosford South, NSW 2250, Australia; tel. (043) 233274; fax (029) 212248

Also available in their countries from the national Oxfams listed on page 127, and in the rest of the world from Oxfam UK and Ireland.

This book is co-published with affiliates of Oxfam International: Community Aid Abroad in Australia; Novib in The Netherlands; Oxfam Canada; Oxfam Hong Kong; and Oxfam New Zealand. Please see page 127 for contact addresses. The book reflects the analysis of a British-based agency working in over 70 countries. It is based on direct programme experience of working with people who have suffered as a result of war but does not cover the whole range of conflicts in the 1990s. It is co-published with other affiliates of Oxfam International as a contribution to international debate about issues of conflict and poverty.

Published by Oxfam (UK and Ireland) 274 Banbury Road, Oxford OX2 7DZ

OX086/RB/97

Printed by Oxfam Print Unit

Oxfam UK and Ireland is a registered charity no. 202918, and is a member of Oxfam International.

Contents

Acknowledgements

Very many Oxfam staff, and members of organisations Oxfam works with, have contributed enormously to this book: too many to mention all of them by name. David Mepham of SaferWorld, and Hugo Slim of Oxford Brookes University gave invaluable comments on the first draft. Many of the ideas in the book have been developed in discussions with some of Oxfam's trustees: Chaloka Beyani, John Borton, Chris Hudson, and Jeremy Swift; and colleagues including David Bryer, Chris Roche, and Nicholas Stockton. For their support during the writing of the book, I should particularly thank Dianna Melrose, Phil Bloomer, and my family.

Edmund Cairns
Oxford, July 1997

Introduction

The trouble came in the morning. Everyone tried to leave as the UNITA soldiers invaded. They shut people in their houses, and then set light to them, burning people alive. Fifty-eight people died.[1]

Filisberto Mateus, master stone-mason working for Oxfam Angola, February 1997

At the beginning of 1997, over 33 million people were refugees or displaced in the 30 or more major armed conflicts being waged throughout the world, from Angola to Liberia, from Sudan to Afghanistan.[2] Though many of these wars are largely ignored by Western media, the deliberate killing of civilians, the rape of women to terrorise whole communities, and the 'cleansing' of ethnic enemies, have become all-too familiar. We live in a world of 'mini-holocausts',[3] in which one side fights the 'other' without mercy. The enemy 'other' is often ethnically defined, but not always: as, for example, the 'political cleansing' of public employees and party supporters in Liberia or Angola.

In many countries, the violence does not end when a 'peace' is agreed. In South Africa or Cambodia or El Salvador, demobilised young men turn to armed banditry to survive; and 'hidden killers' in the form of anti-personnel mines are left in the ground, which kill or maim 200 people a week. Elsewhere, there is not peace but a 'peace process', whereby peace seems to recede like a mirage, while killings continue: in the first two years after Israel and the PLO signed their peace agreement, more than 400 people were killed by extremists on both sides.[4]

Modern conflict — if that is what we should call it — challenges the very distinction between war and peace. It takes place typically not between armies, or even between the army of a state and its armed opposition in some easily-defined guerilla movement. The forces of both government and opposition, from Cambodia to Colombia, blend into illicit business and organised crime. And the blurring of the definition of what is a fighting force makes it more difficult to end a war. Though all the formal 'sides' may agree 'peace', the interests of many individuals, from leaders down, may be to continue the banditry and violent black-marketeering that has become their livelihood.

Yet this increasing complexity need not confuse what policy-makers should be seeking. The aim, though fraught with difficulties, is simple: it is to ensure that the tensions, competition, and change inherent in every society — in themselves no bad thing in an unjust world — can be pursued without a resort to major armed violence. To put it paradoxically, it is to help to make conflict peaceful.

Today, in armed conflicts around the world:

- violence is directed overwhelmingly against civilians;
- violence against civilians is a deliberate strategy, not an accidental side-effect; the frequent purpose is to kill or expel civilians of another group.

Yet most people in countries where war is taking place have no part in these atrocities; some even dare to speak out against the brutality within their society, and take active steps to reduce violence, relieve suffering, and seek reconciliation.

Causes and risks

What really *causes* wars to happen in a particular place at a particular time? Ethnic hatred, poverty, corrupt government, have all been suggested, but no single answer is adequate, and the causes of war are unlikely to be the same in any two countries. And yet there are common features between many of today's wars. First, a ruthless leader who sees political advantage in encouraging and exploiting hatred — hatred which may already exist in latent form, but can be increased to the point, as in Bosnia or Rwanda, where people, often fearful and intimidated themselves, kill their neighbours. Second, the complex and varying mix of pressures which so limit the opportunities open to people that they support the extremism of such leaders. Often with very limited choices, in failed economies, they believe that they no longer have a stake in peace — and can only find one in war.

Sometimes, it is the state itself which wages or sponsors war. But where a collapsing economy means that there are no opportunities to earn a legitimate livelihood, and where a collapsing state offers few services and little security, there may be an overwhelming incentive to co-operate with powerful warlords. So-called 'war economies' offer an income and services to some, while causing death and destruction to many others.

The wars at the end of the twentieth century are taking place in a world which is suffering from unprecedented environmental degradation. More people competing for fewer resources and less useable land will not *inevitably* lead to armed conflict. But greater competition in a degraded environment will increase the *risk*.

The question of what causes any particular war may prove impossible to answer with certainty. But we can be fairly confident in identifying factors which tend to increase the risks of war, and therefore ask how these risks can be reduced. This is an urgent task for people in countries which are now unstable and could either descend into civil war or avoid it. But it is also the responsibility of outsiders, whose actions may be increasing rather than reducing the risks of war — whether by selling arms to governments with little respect for human rights, or, with perhaps better intentions, by supporting economic policies which have insufficient regard for their impact on the poor.

Rights and responsibilities

The years immediately after the Second World War produced a series of new agreements: the Universal Declaration of Human Rights, the Conventions on Genocide and Refugees, the 1949 Geneva Conventions, which, updated by the 1977 Protocols to the Geneva Conventions, give governments who have signed up to these instruments a responsibility to protect civilians from violence during wars, wherever these take place. Yet, at the most conservative estimate, there are at least 170,000 civilian war-fatalities a year,[5] and many more millions of people suffer injury, or destruction of their homes and livelihoods.

This body of international law has laid down certain basic rights for people caught up in a war. Yet what is largely missing is the will to implement and uphold those rights. Rights always imply responsibilities, both for those who claim them and for those who recognise them. For civilians to claim the right to protection places on them an equal responsibility not to infringe the human rights of others. The vast majority of men and women in countries at war are not guilty of human rights abuses, and fully deserve the protection the law affords them. For governments to declare their support for international law implies a willingness on their part not only to maintain the law within their own jurisdiction, but to uphold its principles throughout the world. The vast suffering in current wars is because of the disregard for that law not only by the warring parties themselves, but also by the international community as a whole.

The purpose of this book

Why is Oxfam producing this book at this time? The over-riding reason is because Oxfam is concerned with the relief of suffering: suffering which is caused by long-term poverty (which itself increases the risks of war), and the acute suffering from violence and deprivation caused by war. As the Oxford Committee for Famine Relief, the organisation was founded in 1942 to provide aid for the now-forgotten famine in Nazi-occupied Greece. Since that time, it has worked in many wars: Biafra in the 1960s, Lebanon and many parts of Latin America in the 1970s, Ethiopia, Sudan, and the Middle East in the 1980s, and the Caucasus and the Balkans, Afghanistan, Angola, and Rwanda in the 1990s.

But what has also prompted this book is the more recent realisation that the work of humanitarian agencies has increasingly been used to cover up the failure of governments either to take action to prevent wars starting, or to protect civilians caught up in wars. One of the greatest challenges to all aid agencies is how to provide aid to relieve suffering during war, whilst not prolonging that war; and whilst those who are responsible for protecting civilians fail to do so.

Time and again, emergency aid has become the main, sometimes the only, international response to war. Yet Western governments' funding for humanitarian aid has fallen from US$6 billion in 1994 to US$4.2 billion in 1995, with actual contributions falling well below UN appeal targets for specific emergencies.

Everything which Oxfam does is intended to help people to enjoy ten basic rights,[6] which the organisation set down in 1995 as the summary of what it believed everyone is morally entitled to. All of these rights are also, more or less perfectly, reflected in existing international law. This book expresses the values of one aid agency, based in Britain but with local staff in all the countries in which it works. It is offered as a contribution to the development of the policies which are required, at many different levels, to bring about at least some reduction in the suffering which current wars cause.

In publishing this book, we are acutely conscious that issues of war and peace are extremely complex and open to very varied interpretations. We do not begin to claim we have all the answers. But we are driven by the conviction that the death and suffering caused by armed conflict should no longer be tolerated; and that more can be done to promote people's right to protection from violence.

The main responsibility for civilian death and suffering in wars lies squarely with those who take up arms, and their political masters.

Equally, the main responsibility for building peace lies with the citizens of countries involved in war. And yet governments in other countries share some of the responsibility, if they allow arms sales to the killers, or ignore what is happening in countries where their economic interests are not threatened, or treat refugees and asylum-seekers inhumanely. Western governments, some (particularly members of the Security Council) more than others, have carried some responsibility for civilian suffering. They could choose instead to have a greater role in preventing and relieving it.

Oxfam's experience

This book is based on Oxfam's experience of working with people who have suffered as a result of war. It does not attempt to cover the whole range of conflicts in the 1990s, but to draw on Oxfam's direct programme experience.

Oxfam works in countries at war, and recovering from war, in Eastern Europe, Asia, Africa and Latin America. Much of the experience described in this book comes from a group of countries chosen to show a balance of experience across four continents — Rwanda, Burundi, former Zaire, and Liberia; the countries of former Yugoslavia; Cambodia and Afghanistan; and Colombia. In total, more than ten million people have been forced from their homes[7] in these countries. Finally, through supporting refugees in Britain, Oxfam sees how their suffering seldom ends if they reach the West. In recent years, this suffering has often been prolonged by the changes in asylum procedures and benefit rules for individuals seeking refuge in Britain.

Much of Oxfam's long-term work is supporting communities around the world in their struggle to work themselves out of poverty. Even in the violent 1990s, the 'silent emergency' of poverty kills more than twelve million children — many times more than are killed in war — each year.[8] In many countries, this long-term work is threatened, and overwhelmed, as it was in Rwanda in 1994, by war and the risk of war.

The structure of this book

The rest of the book is set out in seven chapters. Chapter 1, The civilian as target, examines the level of human suffering caused by modern wars. Chapter 2, Flouting the laws of war, describes some of the provisions of international law, and how both combatants and governments around the world are failing to uphold their responsibilities to help to protect civilians. Chapter 3, Guns to kill, considers the problem of the proliferation of weapons, in particular, small arms. Chapter 4, The international response to war, looks at the failure of diplomacy, the tough choices involved in providing humanitarian aid, and the treatment of refugees. Chapter 5, Reducing the risks of war, describes the factors which lead to armed conflict. Chapter 6, Building peace, looks at what makes a society stable, and how local efforts to build and maintain peace can be supported. Finally, Chapter 7, A better way, makes recommendations for four steps which governments and others could take which would reduce the human cost of war.

1 The civilian as target

In July 1995, Hasiba Harbash was living in Srebrenica, having been 'cleansed' from her home village in Bosnia. In 1992, she had watched her mother being taken away to be shot. When Srebrenica fell, she managed to get to Solina, a suburb of Tuzla, where she told an Oxfam worker about the day she last saw her husband:

A Bosnian Serb soldier told my husband and brother-in-law to stand up and go with him ... More soldiers came and told me that the two men would be returned in an hour. But I knew in that moment that I would not see them again.

Half an hour later we were told to board buses. One soldier who was called Georga asked me if I was searching for my husband. And when I explained that he had been taken away, Georga showed me a house which I found was full of about 50 young men, including my husband.

I asked Georga to let me say goodbye to my husband and to allow him to see our baby one last time. He said that my son, who is one year old, could walk to his father but that I could not go to him. I was so afraid that they would keep my child because he is a boy.

I couldn't stop looking at my husband. He looked so pale that he almost seemed dead. He couldn't shout to me but he signalled to me to go to the bus. He kissed his palm and sent us a kiss. That's the last time I saw him ...

The buses had gone. And when I asked the soldier called Georga if there would be others, he told me not to leave that night because all people would be taken to concentration camps. That night all of us laid down on mattresses. There was such a silence ... and then terrible screaming as they took away young women as well.[1]

Hasiba's grandfather was also taken away, and she has not seen him, her husband or brother-in-law since. What happened to the men of her family happened to perhaps 7,000[2] other Muslim men in Srebrenica that week in July 1995.

Hasiba's words remind us that the statistics of war deaths are a measure of infinite numbers of individual experiences of suffering and grief. The annual calculations of Leiden University in the Netherlands estimate that, between mid-1995 and mid-1996, around 169,600 men, women and children were killed in what they define as 'high- and low-intensity conflicts'. The death toll from war in 1994–95 would have been similar,[3] but was hugely increased by the genocide in Rwanda, in which between 500,000 and 800,000 people were killed.

The UN Children's Fund used a broader definition, of 'war-related deaths', in its 1996 *State of the World's Children* report. Looking back over its 50-year history, it presented evidence that around 400,000 people had died as a result of wars in developing countries in every year since 1945. Half a million dead was a bad year; a third of a million, a 'good' year. As UNICEF's head, Carol Bellamy, said: 'Times have changed — and they have not.'[4]

Some researchers estimate that the total death toll is more than double that, at more than a million a year during the 1990s.[5] These different estimates measure a level of human suffering which is hard to comprehend. If current trends continue, over the next decade at least two million people directly, and three and a half million indirectly, will be killed in wars. Surely it must be possible to prevent *some* wars breaking out, to protect *some* civilians, to save *some* of these wasted lives?

Forced to flee

The UN High Commissioner for Refugees referred to the difficulty of quantifying the human suffering from wars in 1995, when her annual report admitted to 'the problem of refugee statistics'.[6] Precision is almost impossible and many people have an interest in either inflating or reducing the figures. But the numbers of men, women, and children forced to flee their countries shows a broad consistency: a plateau of around 15 million a year since 1989 — slightly down at 14 million at the beginning of 1997[7] — significantly higher than in the early 1980s, and dramatically more than in the 1970s. In 1975, the world had 'only' two and a half million refugees.

Many of these 14 million current refugees are not the same people, recounted into each year's new total. When the refugees eventually went home, after long wars in Cambodia, Mozambique or El Salvador, they were 'replaced' by refugees from wars in central Africa or the former Soviet Union. In 1995, there were more than half a million new refugees.[8]

More than half of the world's refugees, almost nine million women, men, and children, have fled from just five conflicts, three of which — those in Rwanda, Liberia and former Yugoslavia — have occurred during the last ten years. The other two huge groups of refugees,

Afghans and Palestinians, come from older, and continuing, conflicts.[9] Some have been refugees for generations. Many Palestinians have lived in refugee camps since 1948; children have been born and brought up knowing nothing of their homeland.

There are still around 2.3 million Afghan refugees from the war which began in 1979. Almost 900,000 live near the north-west frontier of Pakistan.[10] In 1984, Jahan Begum fled from Pul-i-Khumri, in Baglan province in Afghanistan, where her family farmed, growing wheat and millet, and raising some livestock. Thirteen years later, she is now a grandmother, living with her extended family of nine in Akora Khattak refugee camp, about an hour's drive along the road from Peshawar to Islamabad. But she still remembers autumn 1984, when Soviet aircraft and tanks were attacking the hills where she lived, which were controlled by the *mujahideen*:

It took about 20 days to get out of the mountains, travelling at night ... Sometimes we faced government troops, and for two nights we had to hide in the mountains without food. It was September, so it was very cold ... We all travelled together, the whole village. I want to go back to Afghanistan, because even if it is bad there, it is my country.[11]

But in 1997 she is still a refugee. She weaves and teaches weaving to other women, and the cushions which they make are sold to the Oxfam Fair Trade Company for sale in Europe.

The vulnerability of women refugees

A disproportionate number of refugees are women and children; for example, they comprise 80 per cent of all those displaced across former Yugoslavia.[12] In almost every war, refugee women and girls are the 'forgotten majority'.[13]

Unfortunately, when women flee from violence, they do not necessarily escape it as refugees. Almost by definition, refugees often live where law and order has broken down, which can mean 'exposing women to the most barbaric forms of unrestrained male behaviour'.[14] A seemingly neutral technical decision, like where to locate a water tank or toilets in a refugee camp, can be critical to the safety of women threatened by sexual harassment or attack. Looking at refugee camps in Sudan, Kenya, Zimbabwe, and Malawi in 1995, the human-rights expert and Oxfam trustee, Chaloka Beyani, concluded that women often suffered in several specific ways.

Male camp officials quite often demanded sexual favours from women in return for food, or the grant of refugee status to women in their own right. Women who breached camp rules were sometimes offered sexual abuse in lieu of other forms of punishment. The whole camp administration was so dominated by men that women had very little say in matters which affected them as directly as food distribution and personal safety.[15] Services to refugees are not always distributed equally. Three times as many boys as girls receive education while under the care of UNHCR.[16] Women tend to make up around 30 per cent of the population of refugee camps, while only 20 per cent are men. Despite all this, the rights of refugee women are largely ignored in international discussions, not seen as 'human rights', and were left out of the 1993 Vienna Declaration which ended the World Conference on Human Rights.[17]

No refuge at home

For many refugees, their cross-border flight comes after months or even years of trying to find refuge within their own countries. Of the million who fled from Rwanda to Zaire in July 1994, many had been displaced within Rwanda for months because of the fighting between the genocidal former government and the Rwandan Patriotic Front. Some of those from the north of Rwanda had fled to camps around, for instance, Ruhengeri and Bukavu three years earlier, in advance of the RPF's invasion from Uganda in 1990.

The numbers of those who have been forced to flee across national borders are being overtaken by the numbers who are driven from their homes but remain within their countries. Under the relevant international law, only the former are technically 'refugees'.[18] The 1951 Refugee Convention and its 1967 Protocol limit the status of being a refugee to a person who 'owing to a well founded fear of being persecuted ... is outside the country of his [sic] nationality ...'.[19]

The difficulties faced by those who are 'internally displaced' can be even greater than those of refugees abroad. There may not be any well-organised refugee camps to receive them. In Ganda in Angola, they live in a disused coffee factory. Oxfam's Kay Willis worked in Ganda in early 1997:

Once a bustling market town on the railway, and transporting goods to the coast for export, Ganda's industry was paralysed in the war, and its factories left to rot. Today, the only thing the coffee factory is used for is housing the people whose lives have also been paralysed by war — dislocados whose dreams were shattered, and all their potential taken from them. Unable to work or plan for the future, they're reduced to surviving from day to day — depending on hand-outs or foraging around for scraps of food or leaves to eat.

There are 260 families in the old coffee factory. Inside there are small piles of belongings dotted around the smoke-filled, blackened room. Each pile belongs to one family. That is all they own. They huddle round big cooking pots. Most are cooking fuba [maize and water]. The chief shows me how much they have to eat. One small pot of fuba is today's food for five people.[20]

People may move many times over, during long-running wars. In Cambodia, continued Khmer Rouge terrorism serves to keep the number of internally displaced people still above 32,000.[21] Around the world, in January 1997, there were around 19.2 million men, women, and children displaced within their own countries.[22] In 1985, there were half that number.

No refuge abroad

Even if people decide to leave their country to escape the violence of war, they may find no refuge, as other countries are increasingly reluctant to take in refugees.

In Africa, Liberian 'boat people' have been turned away from a number of countries, while refugees from Rwanda and Burundi have faced a declining welcome from traditionally liberal governments like that of Tanzania. At the end of November 1996, Tanzania gave its refugees from Rwanda and Burundi a month to leave the country. Its army turned back the thousands who tried to flee further into Tanzania. One by one, the refugee camps were closed, and people put on the road with their few belongings. Tanzania had become over-burdened by the sheer number of refugees fleeing the wars in the Great Lakes region of central Africa. If countries such as Tanzania are to be able to do more, they deserve greater support from richer donor countries. Tanzania already hosts one refugee for every 80 of its citizens; Liberia one to 25.[23] If Britain hosted a similar ratio to the latter, it would have around two million refugees.

The suffering of host communities

It is not only those forced to leave their homes who suffer; in fact, they are the minority. The communities who receive them may themselves be living in extreme poverty; yet the impulse to help those even worse off is still strong. In late 1996, thousands of people in Kivu offered what little they could, usually a cup of maize or shelter for the night, to those fleeing the fighting in eastern Zaire. Throughout Liberia's war of the 1990s, those who have fled the fighting have been supported by poor rural communities, as well as, in some cases, by international aid.

The suffering of these hosts can be almost as heavy as that of the refugees. A government official in Tanzania described the problems:

..environmental destruction due to the influx of refugees, also the problem of food shortages in the local community, soaring food prices, and the spread of various diseases such as meningitis, malaria, dysentery, venereal diseases.. Our roads and bridges have been badly damaged by heavy trucks ... [24]

The environmental destruction in both Tanzania and former Zaire has included deforestation, water depletion, soil erosion, and problems with the disposal of waste and corpses.

In the town of Goma in Kivu, almost every unskilled job was taken by the refugees who arrived in 1994. Because they could get food and medical care from the aid agencies, they could accept half or a third of the already low wages of local workers. Every morning at seven o'clock, it became a common sight to see the streets leading to Goma thronged with refugees coming for a day's work as maids or labourers. Any international support for people in wars must recognise, and seek to reduce, this potential for tension between refugees and displaced people and their temporary hosts. Too often, this is ignored. As Ian Leggett, Oxfam's manager for east and central Africa, put it in 1996: 'The first group of people who are forgotten are the host communities.'[25]

Counting the cost of war

The destruction and disruption from was can reach almost every corner of a country. Schools and health services are often deliberately targeted to create widespread and lasting damage. Mozambique's war, which ended in 1992, destroyed 70 per cent of the country's schools, cost the country US$15 billion, and has bequeathed to Mozambique its unenviable status as the world's poorest country. In southern Sudan civil war has continued intermittently since the 1950s, and continuously since 1983. The government spends 53 times as much on its military as it does on health; for every million Sudanese there are only ten doctors, and life expectancy is only 36 years.[26]

Since the 1960s, much of the 'developing world' has in fact been developing, at least in economic terms. But countries which have spent most of that time at war have not. On average, the real GDP per capita in developing countries nearly tripled from $915 to $2709 between 1960 and 1993. But in Mozambique, real GDP per capita dropped from $1368 to $640.[27] Sudan, Rwanda, Liberia, Haiti, and Nicaragua all have average per capita incomes lower than they were in 1960.[28]

Killing the civilian

Far more civilians than combatants are killed and injured in armed conflict. Estimates of the proportion of civilians among all those now being killed range upwards from 84 per cent,[29] compared to 15 per cent in the First World War[30] and 65 per cent in the Second.[31] Only atrocities of monumental proportions reach the front pages of the international press. Large-scale violence has become ordinary. It is, as the philosopher Hannah Arendt said of the Nazi holocaust, the 'banality of evil'.

One Oxfam official in Rwanda described one of her experiences of a later genocide like this:

They flushed out and killed seven members of the Tutsi nurse's family ... The victims included a three-year-old boy, his skull split open with a machete blow, and a pregnant woman whose belly was slit open and the unborn baby exposed. We heard the groans, and later the death-rattle, of the elderly mission cook who had been clubbed to the ground.[32]

This barbarism was not unusual in Rwanda in 1994, and is not unusual in wars around the world. As Graca Machel said in November 1996: 'More and more of the world is being sucked into a desolate moral vacuum. This space is devoid of the most basic human values.'[33] In almost all modern wars, what the writer Alex de Waal has called 'conspicuous atrocity' against civilians is used effectively to kill some, terrorise the rest to flee, and undermine the sense of society which could help to build peace again.[34] This is a purposeful targeting of the enemy's 'social capital'; all that helps to bind societies together: family and kinship networks, neighbourhood links, religion, and so on. A climate of fear and suspicion is created; everyone mistrusts everyone else.

Rape as a weapon of war

One of the most chilling indictments of the failure to protect civilians in modern war is the extent to which rape has been systematically used as a weapon of mass terror — with its perpetrators going unpunished. It has been used against thousands of women (and some men) in Algeria,[35] Uganda, Rwanda, Bosnia, Burma, and the Philippines.[36] Precise numbers are almost impossible to discover, but even in 1993 some estimates of the number of women raped in former Yugoslavia were as high as 80,000.[37] Studies in both Mozambique and El Salvador suggested that almost 3 per cent of women had been raped or sexually abused.[38] For long a vicious atrocity to 'reward' fighting men, rape is now commonly used to undermine whole communities through the brutal violation of individual women. Jovanka Stojsavljevic, head of Oxfam in former Yugoslavia during most of the war, explained:

The aim of this [rape] strategy is to humiliate enemy men, and destroy the fabric of the family and society. A raped woman is no longer viewed as 'clean', and often no longer has a place in her family or community.[39]

When the purpose of the war is to destroy the social capital, any symbol of society's cohesion (and women have traditionally been such a symbol) may be attacked.

The 1977 Second Protocol to the Geneva Conventions specifically outlawed rape as a war crime. The International Tribunal in the Hague, charged with prosecuting the war criminals of Rwanda and former Yugoslavia, has now observed that systematic rape may be a crime against humanity.[40] Creating an International Criminal Court, with the capacity to prosecute those who commit crimes against humanity, is one step that could be taken to reduce the incidence of mass rape.

Violence and other burdens on women

It would be beyond the scope of this book to look in detail at the every-day violence against women which most societies seem to tolerate. But it is important to note that there appears to be an increase in domestic violence both during wars, and when soldiers are demobilised. In the long war against apartheid, increased domestic violence was seen on all sides. Dumisa Msezane is a counsellor at People Against Human Abuse in the township of Mamelodi near Pretoria. 'Violence', she explains, 'became a socially sanctioned mechanism for resolving conflict and achieving change. It infiltrated every area of society, including family life.'[41] In the 'peace' which succeeds wars, many men find it difficult to adapt to civilian society, because of the culture of violence which the war encouraged, the lack of economic opportunities, and the fact that they continue to see violence as a 'solution' to their problems.

Wars increase women's burdens in many respects. When men are killed, women often become the single heads of their families,[42] taking responsibility for providing food, clothes, and other needs, as well as caring for children and the elderly.[43] Since the genocide in 1994, a third of Rwanda's households are now headed by women,[44] half of whom are widowed; and a quarter of Colombia's displaced women, numbering around 25,000, are the main wage-earners for their families.[45]

It is often women who have responsibility for what may be difficult and dangerous tasks such as collecting water, food, or fuel. In February 1997, an Oxfam worker met a sixteen-year-old girl, Domingas Mohango, taking water from a well Oxfam had drilled in the Andulo district of Kuito, Angola. Her father had been killed in the war, and she now helps her family by selling chickens in Kuito's market:

The thing that I remember most about the war was getting food. When the city was under siege, we had to walk between 30 and 50 kilometres to collect food from the countryside. We collected sweet potatoes and manioc ... It was very dangerous, and many people were shot or stepped on mines.[46]

However, we should beware of accepting the stereotypes of women as helpless victims of violence and men as the perpetrators of war. Some women are combatants; and while young men may commit acts of violence in war, they are also most at risk of violent death. In a joint study by Oxfam and the aid agency, ACORD, Judy El-Bushra and Eugenia Piza Lopez gave a more realistic analysis:

Women may participate actively in wars as soldiers and support personnel [and] those who do not may still encourage or incite their menfolk to violence. In addition, men as well as women are often unwilling victims of war — killed or maimed, driven from their homes, dragged off reluctantly to fight and be fought.[47]

Child deaths

Children too are acutely vulnerable to the brutality of war. A major UN study on children in wars between 1993 and 1996 concluded that at least 45 per cent of those killed were children.[48] Upwards of half the world's refugees are children.[49] In Colombia, 60 per cent of those who had fled their homes in 1994 were under the age of nineteen.[50] There are also particular ways in which children are abused.

When whole groups are the target, children are not exempt. In early 1994, Rwanda's Radio Mille Collines advised listeners: 'To kill the big rats, you have to kill the little ones.'[51] Perhaps 300,000 'little ones' were killed in Rwanda in the three months from April to June.[52] Over the last ten years, at least two million children have been killed in wars around the world.[53] In 1995, Red Cross workers in Chechnya found that the bodies of some children, who made up 40 per cent of the dead between February and May that year, bore the mark of systematic execution with a bullet through the temple.[54]

Young children are more likely to die from the malnutrition and diseases which war exacerbates. Almost always, the death-rates of children in countries at war, or coming out of wars, are extremely high. Diarrhoea, malaria, measles, and respiratory infections often kill children already weakened by malnutrition. In Angola, Afghanistan, Sierra Leone, and Mozambique, between a quarter and a third of children die before they reach the age of five.[55]

Perhaps even more than adults, children suffer the trauma of war. As the shells and snipers' bullets fell about them in 1993, two-thirds of Sarajevo's children surveyed by UNICEF had been in a situation where they thought they were about to die.[56] In Rwanda's 1994 genocide, almost 80 per cent of children lost members of their immediate families, and in more than a third of these cases, the children witnessed the murders.[57] One nine-year-old Liberian girl described how she saw her uncle die:

They shot my uncle in the head and killed him. Then they made my father take his brains out and throw them into some water nearby. Then they made my father undress and have an affair with a decaying body. Then they raped my cousin who was a little girl of nine years old.[58]

The trauma from rape may be among the longest to heal, according to evidence from Uganda which suggests that girls tend to suffer even longer-lasting psychological problems than boys.[59] Though boys are sometimes raped and forced into prostitution during wars, teenage girls are far more likely to suffer this fate; perhaps because they are assumed to be less likely to be carriers of HIV than are adult women.[60]

Together with the lack of reproductive health services, sexual violence means that girls face particular dangers in many modern wars, though boys remain more likely to be killed or maimed. Though, of course, everyone suffers if they have poor or no health services, the need of girls — and women — for reproductive care makes them more vulnerable.

Child killers

Of course, children are not all innocent victims of war: in Rwanda, 40 children are facing trial for genocide.[61] Something which *is* new in many modern wars is the widespread use of children as soldiers. The use of tens of thousands of child-soldiers is well-documented in at least 24 wars of the 1990s.[62] One estimate has put the number worldwide at as high as 200,000.[63] In many cases,[64] children voluntarily join fighting forces in order to gain protection from the violence around them, or just to obtain a regular supply of food.[65]

In 1995 in Sierra Leone, the Revolutionary United Front raided villages to capture children for its ranks, and forced them to witness or take part in the execution of their families. Outlawed and brutalised, and often fed crack cocaine and other drugs, the children were then led to neighbouring villages to continue killing.[66]

Psychosocial suffering

Only recently has the level of psychosocial suffering from war been widely recognised. In Mozambique, 44 per cent of women witnessed a murder, a quarter were separated from their children, and almost a third were tortured.[67] The experiences of men, women, and children caught up in war include personal injury, loss of family members and friends, loss of home and belongings, and loss of livelihood, which, depending on cultural and social values, may have significance beyond its economic value. Life may lose its meaning and logic, people's beliefs and ideologies may be undermined. They may witness or be forced to watch or participate in atrocities, or themselves experience torture or rape. Survivors may feel guilty simply about their own survival; or may suffer the guilt of wrongdoing or failing to protest at others' actions. The extraordinary stressful, uncontrollable, terrifying experiences of war may represent major traumas which have implications for the psychological and social well-being of survivors.

Something can be done

Images of atrocities in the former Yugoslavia and Rwanda have become part of our mental map in the 1990s. In Bosnia, if not in Rwanda, coverage in the media eventually helped to push Western governments to take the diplomatic and military action in summer 1995 which ended the war. Other wars are less well-reported, but no less destructive. The focus of the international media on Colombia, Liberia, Angola, Sudan or Afghanistan, has been intermittent; yet, together, these wars have accounted for around 4.7 million deaths in recent years.[68]

Where this catalogue of civilian suffering has been widely reported, it has stimulated revulsion at the level of violence and the widespread demand that 'something must be done' to end it. The anger of people in the 1990s at what happened to Hasiba Harbash's family, and thousands more, in Srebrenica was the same human impulse which, 50 years earlier, had prompted the formulation of much of modern international law in the aftermath of the Nazi Holocaust. Later chapters of this book will set out the 'something' which we believe can be done to reduce the human cost of war. But first, in chapter 2 we will look at how and why civilians' most basic legal rights to protection from violence are being violated in wars throughout the world.

2 Flouting the laws of war

The violence described in the previous chapter violates 'the right to life, liberty and security of person' laid down in the Universal Declaration of Human Rights, 50 years old in 1998, as well as several of what used to be called the 'laws of war', now generally referred to as international humanitarian law (IHL). When governments sign up to the various conventions and protocols which make up IHL, they accept an obligation to help in upholding these laws wherever they are being violated. The claim that something can and should be done to reduce the suffering of civilians in war is based on firm legal grounds. It represents a challenge to the international community to uphold what most people, and most governments, have agreed, for nearly half a century, are universal human rights.

Since almost all current wars are civil wars, the more detailed relevant rights are those relating to wars 'not of an international character', as the 1949 Geneva Conventions put it. Article 3, which is common to all the 1949 Geneva Conventions, sets down the minimum rights for civilians, which are universal and absolute, and can never be suspended[1] — and which governments[2] have a responsibility to uphold, worldwide. Civilians, it states, should be 'treated humanely' and protected from 'violence to life and person ... [and] outrages to personal dignity, in particular humiliating and degrading treatment'.

The Second Protocol to the Conventions, agreed in 1977, which deals entirely with 'non-international' wars, repeats these basic rights. It applies to all civilians as long as they are not taking 'a direct part in hostilities'. Its Article 4 specifically outlaws rape and threats to commit any prohibited act. Article 13 outlaws 'acts or threats of violence the primary purpose of which is to spread terror among the civilian population'. Article 14 then sets out an unconditional prohibition against starvation and against the destruction of food, agricultural areas, crops, livestock, and water supplies.

Minimum standards

These rights set down in 1949 and 1977 were not seen as ideal standards to aspire to, but as the absolute minimum protection for civilians, to prevent the worst excesses of war. If there is little that the international community can do to end the long-running wars in southern Sudan, Burundi or Afghanistan, it still has a responsibility to protect the civilian victims of those, and more recent, wars.

In Rwanda in 1994, given the unwillingness of UN member states to reinforce the depleted peace-keeping force, the victory of the Rwandan Patriotic Front was probably the only realistic way for the genocide to be halted. But around 800,000 people were killed in the three months between the start of the massacres on 6 April, and the victory of the RPF in early July. During this time, the tiny UN force, cut by the Security Council in April, was able to save thousands of lives. For example, Rwandan nationals who had fled to the Amahoro stadium and a nearby hospital were protected by a single armoured personnel carrier, a demoralised Belgian battalion, and an under-equipped, below-strength unit from Bangladesh. If the UN force had not been cut, and if the reinforcements which the Security Council approved in May had not arrived too late, it is almost certain that UNAMIR could have saved thousands more lives. Under the Geneva Conventions, and the 1948 Genocide Convention, the governments of the world had a responsibility to enable UNAMIR to save the lives of civilians. Had the UN been able to act more assertively before April 1994, in response to the many warnings from concerned observers, perhaps most of the deaths might have been prevented.

The rights listed above are absolute for all civilians in all wars; though parts of international law do recognise a balance between the rights of civilians and the military purpose of the combatants. For example, the ban on the forced displacement of civilians is balanced against the needs of the warring parties to pursue their ends. Similarly, when governments negotiated the Second Protocol in the 1970s, they left access for humanitarian supplies conditional on the consent of the government concerned.

However, international law develops by custom as well as agreement, and the law in this area has been influenced significantly by a series of resolutions by the UN Security Council since April 1991. In that month, the Gulf War had just ended, and the Security Council authorised the US-led coalition to use military power to ensure humanitarian aid got through to the Kurds of northern Iraq. The lack of consent on the part of the government in Baghdad was not allowed to be an obstacle in this instance.

Since then, a succession of Security Council decisions, including action on Somalia in 1992 and in Albania in 1997, although the motives may have been mixed and the approach inconsistent, have effectively placed the rights of civilians above all else. Indeed, the sovereignty of the state, or the authority of the warring party, has become conditional on its respect for these rights. It has been clearly recognised that the individual civilian in a war can claim both protection and relief from her or his state, or the occupying power in her or his country. And if that protection or relief is not forthcoming, the international community has a duty to do what it can to provide them. This legal development is both welcome and significant.

Longer-standing international agreements define rights to much of what wars destroy. The Universal Declaration and the subsequent seven great international instruments concerning civil and political rights, economic, social and cultural rights, racial discrimination, genocide, torture, the status of women and the rights of children, present a range of indivisible rights, almost all of which require a peaceful environment if they are to be fully realised. The Universal Declaration[3] laid down that everyone has a right to sufficient food, and to the highest attainable standard of health, which is generally taken to include access to such things as clean water. The later International Covenant on Economic, Social and Cultural Rights[4] endorsed this. In 1993, governments gathered at the UN's World Conference on Human Rights in Vienna to repeat such commitments, and make some important additions. The rights of women, including the right to live free from violence, were specifically recognised for the first time.

Disregard of international law

The longer the list of international agreements on the rights of civilians, the more glaring the gap between legal theory and reality. The fiftieth anniversary of the United Nations in 1995 was marked by a range of books arguing that the moral and legal consensus which had emerged 50 years before had collapsed. The Nazi Holocaust (the first named 'genocide'), and the enormous suffering of civilians in the Second World War, had prompted most of the international law outlined above, as well as the Genocide Convention in 1948, and the Refugee Convention in 1951. Then, it seemed that the world had finally been provoked, as it had not been by the genocide of two and a half million Armenians in 1915–21, or any previous atrocity, to say 'never again'. The new United Nations, replacing the League of Nations, was supposed to be at the centre of a new rule of international law.

There is a danger that the word 'genocide' can be too readily applied, so that its horror is devalued. What happened in Rwanda in the second quarter of 1994 may be the only indisputable example of genocide since 1945 — though not all governments accepted that at the time. But, whatever terminology is used, the 22 million deaths in wars since the Second World War are a measure of the failure to bring about the 'peace and security' which the UN Charter was intended to ensure.

War against the 'other'

Barbarity is not a new phenomenon; terrorising civilians has been part of war throughout recorded history: as in the 'bellum romanum' of medieval Europe, 'in which no holds were barred and all those designated as enemy, whether bearing arms or not, would be indiscriminately slaughtered'.[5] But there was also the bellum hostile, war with restraint, based on the same principles which half a millennium later informed the first Geneva Convention in 1864.

Attacks on civilians by their governments have been part of the 'counter-insurgency' tactics of colonial and independent rulers for much of this century. In the 1970s and 1980s, as the USSR and US competed to support sympathetic governments and rebel movements, the US applied a doctrine of 'low-intensity conflict' from the Philippines to Central America, in which para-militaries, vigilantes, and civilian groups were armed against Marxist guerillas. Most of the killings of civilians in Colombia are still carried out by such paramilitary groups, often with the army's involvement, though the guerrillas also target civilians, who say they feel 'in the middle of two fires'.

During the Cold War, many civil wars were presented as ideological, and, for all their brutality, their real purpose did appear to be the removal of the government for the alleged benefit of the whole population. For this reason, the Viet Cong fought the South Vietnamese government, and the Tigrayan People's Liberation Front eventually overthrew Ethiopia's Marxist-Leninist dictatorship of Colonel Mengistu, the Derg.

There now seems to be an emerging trend in the very purpose of many — though not all — current armed conflicts. Speaking in Tuzla, in Bosnia, a few days after Srebrenica fell in July 1995, the UN High

Commissioner for Refugees, Sadako Ogata, observed that 'ethnic cleansing' was the purpose, not just the result, of Bosnia's war.[6] Many modern wars are fought in order not to change the government within an existing state, but to carve out a new state or quasi-state on behalf of only one particular ethnic group; or to 'cleanse' the state of all but that group, usually for the benefit of a comparatively small elite within the group.

For Cambodia's Khmer Rouge, the control of people and natural resources has long been a prime objective. But in other cases, the aim of warring factions, from the Balkans to former Zaire, is not to control a population but to exclude it — to remove the 'others' from a territory, by killing them, destroying property and livelihoods, and employing terrorist tactics such as rape and torture, in violation of international law.

Beyond the ethnic

The 'other' is not, of course, always defined by ethnicity. In the Colombian army's training manuals in 1995, it was civilians in guerrilla-controlled areas who were defined as the 'enemy'[7]. In Angola, people are targeted because they are the supporters, however humble, of political opponents. Virgilio Joya runs Oxfam's projects in the town of Ganda:

People here ... are of the same ethnic group. They have everything to share. But they don't trust each other. People who support the government say that UNITA's army are the killers. And people in UNITA's areas say the same about the government.[8]

According to one Ganda priest, José Ukulatchiali, between 500 and 1000 people were murdered, by both government and opposition supporters, in the two years to 1994. They were killed just because they were known to have voted the 'wrong way' in the 1992 election.

Civilian complicity?

While most civilians in modern wars remain non-combatants, some do not. They may have virtually no choice; caught between the cross-fire and suspicion of government forces and guerillas, their only hope of protection is to decide 'which side they are on', or to take up arms to defend themselves.

The question of civilian complicity in war is an extremely difficult one. Tens of thousands of Rwandan Hutu, perhaps several hundred thousand, were involved in the 1994 genocide, and made up a significant minority of the 1.2 million Rwandan refugees who fled into eastern

Zaire. In the war in Bosnia from 1992-5, there were examples of Serb, Croat, and Muslim civilians forcing their neighbours out of their homes, and of civilians blocking aid convoys destined for their ethnic enemies. In the 'cleansing' of Srebrenica, Bosnian Serb women stoned buses carrying away the women whose men had just been taken away to be shot.[9] It is easy to think that all civilians collude with the barbarity of modern war. The reality is less simple but rather more positive. (Some examples of active peace-making are given in Chapter 6.)

In a society at war, most people identify, to a greater or lesser degree, with one side or another. People's identities, as Hutu or Tutsi, Serb or Croat, are at least a factor in most current wars. Yet most people are not party to, or responsible for, the massacres of civilians or the rape of women. To suggest that almost everyone is guilty, is to reduce the responsibility of those who actually kill, rape, or give the orders to do so. The bombing of Dresden in 1945 may have been an atrocity, but responsibility for it lies with those who ordered it, and carried it out, not with all those who supported the war against Nazi Germany.

Just wars

Almost all cultures have developed principles to help to determine whether war can be justified. What in Western philosophy has been termed the theory of 'a just war' is based on the premise that the tough ethical choice in some circumstances may be to fight to reduce enormous injustice and suffering. In all circumstances, the idea of a just war has excluded unrestrained 'total war' which treats civilians and combatants alike.

Force, 'just war' theorists would argue, may sometimes be necessary to stop or reduce the violence of an aggressor or tyrant. Poor people and social movements may resort to violence, and would claim the right to do so when they are suffering physical attack and systematic human rights abuse, and lack any peaceful or democratic avenues for change. Thus, wars of liberation or self-defence are often claimed as examples of 'just wars'.

One problem is that these justifications can be exploited by every fighting force seeking to portray its war, however brutal, as morally justified. Most commentators would agree that any violence is *unjust* unless the perpetrators are themselves being subjected to gross violation of their human rights, and all non-violent means of bringing about change have been tried and failed. The controlling authority — government or rebel — would need to have clearly demonstrated its unwillingness or inability to end acute civilian suffering before any armed opposition to it could be justified in any way.

Any credible concept of 'just war' must have a heavy presumption against war, and provide demanding criteria that must be met before a resort to violence can be justified. These would include whether the violence would have a reasonable chance of success, in a reasonable time, and whether it would be genuinely supported by the people it purported to be saving from greater suffering. Though fighters and their leaders may define themselves as guardians of their communities, this does not guarantee that in fact they have such legitimacy or are in any way accountable to the community whose interests they claim to advocate. As the head of Oslo's renowned Peace Research Institute put it in 1997:

People continue to die in wars that are fought only to decide which unrepresentative group of people should control a given area.[10]

'Just war' theory very clearly condemns unrestrained violence, in whatever 'cause'. Violence can never be justified if it is disproportionate to the suffering which it aims to reduce, and should be the minimum necessary to achieve the 'just' goal, and fully respect humanitarian and human rights law. Very few, if any, current wars would appear to meet these broad principles.

By definition, atrocities can never be part of a 'just war'. For those who would define the armed fight against fascism in Europe in the twentieth century as a 'just war', atrocities committed by the Allies were still inexcusable, shaming a just cause. More recent wars against the evils of apartheid, poverty or social exclusion have presented complex ethical choices for those committed to the struggle against poverty and injustice. But what is clear is that nothing can justify the violation of civilians' rights. Violence against those who should be protected destroys any legitimacy the fighters may claim to have. The Red Cross, the official guardian of the Geneva Conventions, does an impressive if daunting job around the world of trying to promote this message to soldiers, across cultural divides.

War and famine

Through deliberate strategies to fan famine or disease, or the diversion of aid to fighters, men, women and children are often denied their most basic rights. Scorched earth policies to starve civilians are as old as the history of war. The long Nazi retreat through the Soviet Union in 1944–5, for example, was accompanied by the widespread destruction of anything which local people or the reconquering Red Army could use. In the 1980s, the Ethiopian government devastated hundreds of thousands of acres of Tigray's food-producing land in its war against the region's rebels.[11]

Famine frequently kills more people than war-related violence. But often famine is not so much the result of natural disaster, but of war. In Biafra in 1968, northern Ethiopia in 1984–5, Mozambique in 1986 and 1992-3, southern Sudan in 1988-90 and 1992–4, and Somalia in 1992–3, drought, crop failure, and war have combined to create famines which have together killed millions. Angola, Liberia, and southern Sudan have all experienced major famines in the 1990s which were unrelated to drought.[12] In East Timor, about one in three people died from famine after Indonesia's annexation of the territory. The upheaval suffered by the civilian population, their inability to plant their crops, and the total destruction of the economy, led to widespread starvation and related diseases. Many observers believe that the famine was a deliberate strategy on the part of the Indonesian government.

Perhaps the most influential book on famine in the last ten years, *Hunger and Public Action*, by Amartya Sen and Jean Drèze, describes seven ways in which wars make countries more vulnerable to famine. They range from the immediate destruction of crops to the suppression of a free media and civil rights, which, Sen and Drèze argued, make governments more likely to use famine as part of their own counter-insurgency strategy, and less likely to take steps to prevent it.[13]

In southern Sudan, Cambodia, Zaire, and Burundi, and throughout the war in Bosnia, the warring sides have restricted the access of humanitarian agencies to people in need of emergency aid. In Sarajevo, water supplies were deliberately destroyed in residential neighbourhoods. By the end of 1995, 30 per cent of the pumping system and 60 per cent of the water-mains had been ruined.[14] In Chechnya, Zaire, Burundi and Rwanda, Liberia and Sierra Leone, Afghanistan and Angola — indeed, in almost every current war — violence against aid workers, and the misappropriation of aid, has sometimes halted relief operations altogether.

Values for the next century?

For tens of millions of people, the end of the twentieth century is a time of war, not a time of peace. It is fitting to ask what values we want upheld in the next century. For Oxfam, they are that everyone has a basic right to protection from violence, to the basic needs of life, to earn a living, and have a say in the future. It works to help people to enjoy these rights, and to do so in a socially responsible way. For tens of millions of people, war destroys the possibility of peaceful development.

The argument that civilians have some rights in wars is firmly based on international law. Despite the involvement of some 'civilians' in fighting, most people affected by modern wars are not combatants and therefore deserve the protection which international law aims to provide. Why they do not get that protection, and what can be done to ensure they do, is the subject of the rest of this book. Perhaps self-evidently, the warring leaders themselves have the greatest responsibility to reduce the suffering of civilians under their control. Yet the international community also has a responsibility, both to uphold international law, and to reduce the capacity of the killers to kill. The high number of casualties in wars around the world is directly related to the availability of modern weapons. Chapter 3 looks at the double cost of the proliferation of arms — the direct killing and the waste of poor countries' resources — and asks how new international policies could help to reduce it.

3 Guns to kill

Among the reasons why so many civilian men, women, and children are killed and injured in current wars is simply the development, and proliferation, of modern small arms: basic, brutally effective — and cheap.[1] In Liberia, for example, a Kalashnikov can be bought for US$10. Since 1947, 55 million of these weapons have been sold around the world.[2] Modern, light weapons no longer need grown men to operate them. A Kalashnikov or an American M16 can be stripped and reassembled by a child of ten[3] — making the use of child soldiers a viable military strategy.

The easy availability of modern weapons tends not only to increase the risks of war, but the civilian suffering caused, and also tends to prolong the conflict. Automatic rifles and landmines are far more destructive than even the weapons of the comparatively recent past.[4] Because of the damage that such weapons can do, they tend to increase the cost of post-war reconstruction:[5] the World Bank expects the bill for rebuilding Bosnia to exceed US$ 4 billion.[6]

Although in Rwanda's genocide the instrument of death was often a machete, the killers also used automatic weapons to round up their victims before execution. The use of automatic small arms, including grenades, which were not widely available in poor countries 50 years ago, has transformed the way people fight, and the numbers who are killed.

Long-running wars rely on a steady supply of arms and, perhaps even more so, ammunition. Blocking the flow of ammunition can sometimes have a huge effect in reducing violence. In 1993 and early 1994, the ill-fated UNOSOM mission in Somalia enforced an effective arms embargo in the lower Juba in the south of the country. Fighters began discarding their guns, fewer Somalis were being killed, and agencies like Oxfam could help people in comparative peace. After the UN left the area, the trade in ammunition restarted, and the local struggle for power again became more violent.

Once wars are over, many weapons do not lie idle but, as in South Africa or Nicaragua, are used by criminal gangs in bus robberies, kidnapping, extortion, and street thefts. Not only are there often large numbers of arms in countries emerging from war, but these weapons are, inevitably, in the hands of young men, ex-fighters who may have grown up in an intensified culture of violence during the war, and now have no opportunities to earn a living. There may be little real peace after the war is over.

The international arms trade

Few of today's wars are fought in major arms-producing states. Even in the former Yugoslavia, which had built up a significant arms industry, the wars were fought with the help of large supplies of arms from several other countries. At different levels of legality, former East German arms flowed into Croatia, and guns from Lebanon's civil war, paid for by Iran and other Muslim governments, supplied Bosnia's government.[7] Since then, arms sent to the region have included those provided by the US to the Bosnia-Croatian Federation. The ready availability of arms in current wars is therefore largely because of the ease of transferring them around the world. And a significant proportion of them are transferred to countries which are unstable and whose governments can not afford to buy them if they are to effectively tackle poverty. In 1994, 71 per cent of all arms transferred went to developing countries, including in the Middle East.[8]

Many of the wars of the 1970s and 1980s saw the massive arming of poor countries with automatic weapons by the Cold War super-powers. Soviet arms flooded into wars from Ethiopia to Angola. The US arming of vigilantes and paramilitaries in 'low-intensity conflicts' bequeathed to many countries a vast proliferation of small arms, outside the control of the military, facilitating widespread violence and banditry.

Though the total world arms market collapsed by more than a half from the late 1980s to 1992,[9] and has not significantly recovered, two-thirds of the fall in trade was accounted for by the former Soviet bloc, and most of the rest has been in major weapons systems, not the small arms used in current civil wars.[10] Up to 90 per cent of the casualties in today's wars are caused by small arms and light weapons — essentially portable anti-aircraft guns and everything smaller.[11]

The ending of the Cold War produced stockpiles of old armaments to sell; and, as major markets shrunk, this merely served to increase the commercial incentive to sell new arms to developing countries. Strategic interests remained significant in the post-Cold-War world; for example, the US sent helicopters to the Mexican government to fight in Chiapas, and France supplied weapons to the former governments of Rwanda and Zaire. In the early 1990s, export controls collapsed in some of the former Soviet bloc countries, leaving the Czech Republic and Ukraine as reportedly among the centres of the international illegal arms market.

There is some irony in the fact that the five permanent members of the UN Security Council, whose mission is to preserve 'international peace and security', supply most of the world's arms: 86 per cent in 1993.[12] With Germany, these five — the UK, US, France, Russia and China — account for up to 90 per cent of total arms sales of around US$30 billion a year, the level at which the world's arms trade has stabilised since 1992.[13]

Britain is second only to the US as an arms exporter, with a 25 per cent share of the legal global market.[14] And British arms have gone to some of the poorest and least stable regions of the world. Between 1990 and 1994, they made up 13 per cent of total arms exports to sub-Saharan Africa.[15] In the 1990s, British companies have allegedly been involved in the supply of arms to the UNITA rebels in Angola, who plunged the country back into war after rejecting the 1992 election results.[16] The tenth poorest country in the world, according to the UN in 1996,[17] Angola received US$7.3 billion of arms in the seven years to 1994.[18] British Sterling sub-machine guns were among weapons collected by the UN in El Salvador. In 1996, the British company Miltec was revealed to have been sending arms to the former Rwandan government, in contravention of the UN embargo, through a loophole in the UK law.

Arms production provides employment, whether in the West, China, former Communist countries, or countries like South Africa, Brazil, Malaysia, and India with their own newer arms industries. Argentina, Mexico, Chile, Pakistan, and Zimbabwe all have arms exports of over US$10 million a year.[19] In Britain, defence-related industry still employed 350,000 people in 1995, though the number of jobs had fallen by 44 per cent since 1987, a trend which is broadly in line with all other major arms exporters.[20] Only a quarter of these British jobs are related to military exports.[21]

However, the defence industry tends to be more capital-intensive than most manufacturers of civilian products, and so investment in arms manufacture does not result in the creation of many new jobs. In Britain, government subsidies to support arms exports have effectively been at the expense of support for civil exports, and so not necessarily good for 'UK plc' at all. The Arms Control and Disarmament Agency reported that arms made up 2.4 per cent of British exports in the first half of the

1990s, but cost, on average, 34 per cent of the support for export guarantees.[22] Government support for exports has taken the form of, among other things, overseas marketing promotions, export credit guarantees, and 'offset' arrangements.

Regulation

Few would now deny that the proliferation of small arms, as well as weapons of mass destruction, should be stopped. More specifically, there is an increasing desire in many arms-producing countries to see a better regulated market, which would help to prevent arms getting to those who wish to use them against civilians.

The covert nature of the supposedly legal trade, and the lack of open governmental control, has recently been exposed in several arms-producing countries, including Britain, the US, and France. Both in the US and the EU, together accounting for 80 per cent of the legal market, there are steps to establish codes of conduct which could bring effective regulation on internationally-agreed terms. In June 1997, the US House of Representatives supported this for the first time, and a number of EU governments are now convinced of the need to turn the very broad principles for arms exports which they agreed in 1992 into an effective regulatory framework. Costa Rica's former President Dr Oscar Arias, and six other Nobel Peace Laureates, have recently argued that these regional developments must lead on to an international code applying to all countries.[23]

For light weapons, only about 45 per cent of the trade is legal. The problem of control is made more complex by the large quantities of arms traded in the massive 'black', or more accurately, 'grey' market in weapons which leave a Western country legally, with an apparently bona fide certificate to show their 'end user', and then gradually become less and less legal as they are sold on, perhaps several times, to users which the original exportinggovernment knows nothing of, and makes no effort to find out about. There is, in fact, a comparatively small market which is completely outside the knowledge and therefore beyond the possible tighter control of governments.

Western arms exports, especially small arms, have always 'trickled down' to users who have not been the ones exporting governments intended. This has partly been because of inevitable difficulties in tracking arms around the world, but partly because exporting countries have paid less attention to where their small arms end up than they have to the destination of their tanks and combat jets. Up to 70 per cent of the US$8 billion of arms sent along the arms pipeline from Karachi to the Afghan *mujahideen* leaked out into the hands of criminals, and people fighting different wars from the one the US and other suppliers intended.[24] Many of the weapons transferred from the US to the *mujahideen* since the mid-1980s are now on display in arms bazaars in and around Pakistan's North West Frontier province, being bought for use in Pakistan, Afghanistan, and India. Along the way, they increase the violence in Afghanistan's neighbours. What is called in Pakistan the 'Kalashnikov culture' has helped to increase the number of armed robberies, kidnappings for ransom, and gun battles between rival groups. In a six-day period in June 1997, 58 people were killed in Pakistan by small arms in sectarian and criminal violence.[25]

After the end of the Cold War, Western governments had little interest in tight control, and the former Soviet Union no ability to exercise it. The American weapons sent to Somalia's President Barre, and the Soviet ones to President Mengistu in Ethiopia, all found their way into the hands of Somali warlords after the fall of the Ethiopian communist government in 1991.

Many of the guns used in Colombia's conflict, in which so far more than 100,000 men, women, and children have died,[26] come directly from the vast black market in Nicaragua, El Salvador, and Panama, and originated from US military aid to Nicaragua's *contras* and others in the 1980s.[27] Colombia provides a classic example of how loosely producer governments monitor the end-use to which their weapons are put, and how much such lack of control is against their own interest. When almost 200 guns were seized from one drug baron, almost all of them had been legally imported from the US and registered by the government's own arms industry, INDUMIL.[28] It seems that foreign suppliers make no effective attempt to prevent the flow of imported arms between the state, *paras, narcos*, guerillas, common criminals[29] — or the 100,000 private security officers who guard wealthy Colombians and their property.[30]

Much the same could be said, in most countries, about the sale of equipment which can be used in battle, and also to 'restrain' crowds and prisoners (so-called 'dual-use' arms). As Chapter 5 will argue, the abuse of human rights lies at the root of many current conflicts; regulating the trade in the tools of repression is also very necessary. The main suppliers of this equipment are the US, the UK, France, Germany, and Russia.[31]

What President Eisenhower christened the 'military-industrial complex' 40 years ago seems as powerful as ever, on the evidence of

President Clinton's decision in early 1997 to supply sophisticated aircraft to Chile, against the advice of the US State Department. As the EU moves towards an increasingly integrated defence industry, how it responds to the competing pressures from manufacturers and from the greater demands for tighter regulation will be an indication of whether there can be, as the British Foreign Secretary Robin Cook has suggested, a more ethical foreign policy. One of the positive developments of 1997 has been the EU's agreement in June to a Programme For Preventing and Combating Illicit Trafficking in Conventional Arms, which promises a tougher and more coordinated approach by police and customs officers in member states, and greater support to countries coming out of war to tackle the problem of disarmament. Among other things, this would include funding the purchase and destruction of weapons.

Tighter regulation of exports is only half of the solution. By itself, it does not deal with the arms recycled between countries, as in Central America or the Horn of Africa. The whole question of what to do with existing arms is a pressing one. One answer is the 'security first' approaches to post-war reconstruction which have recently been adopted, in which economic aid is focused on re-integrating demobilised fighters and the destruction of arms; for example, the La Flamme de Paix operation in Mali, in which nearly 3,000 small arms were destroyed in Timbuktu in 1996. Another answer is tighter border controls; joint commissions have been set up by the governments of Mali, Niger, and Burkina Faso to prevent cross-border arms smuggling. Recent studies of effective demobilisation in Africa and Central America clearly suggest that disarmament is an essential pre-requisite, but that a wide range of additional support for demobilised soldiers is needed, including counselling, technical and managerial training and advice, provision of tools, credit facilities, and the construction of houses.

As the fighters in El Salvador were demobilised at the end of its long conflict, each had to hand in one weapon; yet 200,000 guns still remain in circulation. 'Buy-back' can be vital, but is not simple. It has to be limited to a few days in each site, to avoid some people simply handing in old weapons to get money to buy new ones. Since so many countries are awash with weapons, even after 'buy-back' programmes, much of the focus of the tighter international regulation must be on ammunition, if it is to be effective. The industrial-scale production of ammunition is limited to a few countries, and, because ammunition has to be packed with bulky protection for reasons of safety, it is often less easy to conceal than weapons.

Landmines

In the mid-1990s, landmines, probably more than any other weapon, have become a symbol of the way in which civilian women, men and children are the main victims of modern war.[32] Mines, left in the ground long after 'peace' has been declared, make no distinction between the footsteps of a soldier or a child. The international campaigning of organisations like the Red Cross, and individuals like Princess Diana, have helped to create a public revulsion against landmines, in many countries.

Since 1975, more than one million people have been landmine victims.[33] Now they kill or maim around two thousand people a month, most of them women and children, almost all of them civilians. Three countries — Cambodia, Angola, and Afghanistan — between them account for 85 per cent of all the world's landmine casualties.[34] Other countries where civilians face great risk are Somalia, Mozambique, Iraq, and Laos.[35] And although the war in Vietnam ended many years ago, mines and unexploded bombs continue to kill and injure civilians.[36]

Berta Ngheve is a 23-year old Angolan mother of two. She now works as a tailor. One day in 1994 her life changed:

I was walking to Kuito with my sister to get food from the World Food Programme when I stepped on a mine. I didn't know the path was dangerous. The main road had been closed but there was a small path to the left of the road that people were taking to travel to Kuito.

It happened on 12 January 1994. I heard a lot of noise, and then there was silence. A second later when I looked at my leg, I realised what had happened. At that time, I didn't feel any pain ...

Life is more difficult now. I can't work as quickly as I used to. Everything is harder — getting water, collecting firewood, getting food.[37]

Berta's experience is just one of 5,000 similar cases of people maimed every year in Angola.[38] Oxfam and other aid agencies have lost their own staff members to mines. In Mozambique, an explosion in 1993 killed Oxfam's Illidio Candiero and severely injured his colleague, Agostinho Chirrine, four months after the peace treaty had been signed. In Bosnia and Georgia, UN peace-keepers have been killed by mines.

Long after a war is over, mines — and other unexploded ordnance — keep killing. Just the threat of this is enough to make huge tracts of agricultural land unusable, and force people to remain as refugees when they could otherwise go home. In much of Cambodia, the level of fighting has reduced. But Hun Peun, a 45-year-old man still living in a settlement for the displaced near Bavel, explained the problem to an Oxfam worker in early 1997:

Since the local Khmer Rouge went over to the government [in 1996], I'd go back to the village tomorrow, but there are mines. Animals have been killed by them. And some displaced people have tried to return and been killed by mines. I saw the bodies being carried along this road. The best help anyone could give us is to get those mines cleared.[39]

In Cambodia's Battambang province, a third of the land is still too polluted by mines to be habitable.[40] Every month in Cambodia, 300 amputations are carried out on mines victims.[41]

Landmines can be detected and removed, but the process is slow, dangerous, and costly. A mine which can be bought for a dollar can cost more than US$300 to clear.[42] The safest and most effective way is still to lie on your stomach and prod the earth inch by inch with a metal rod.[43] It can take a day or more for a skilled person to clear 50 square metres.[44] At the present rate of clearance, mines laid at the end of this century will still be killing and maiming people into the middle of the next.

Landmines are an effective means of terrorising civilian populations. As one Khmer Rouge general put it, a mine is 'ever courageous, never sleeps, never misses'.[45] As for legitimate military purposes, there is now a growing debate between army officers in Britain, the United States, and elsewhere on whether landmines provide any net military benefit at all.

The increasing public intolerance of landmines has driven more than 80 governments to ban them. South Africa and the UK were among the countries to introduce a ban in 1997. Chapter 7 suggests that a major step can be achieved by the signing of an international treaty committing its signatories to a total ban by the year 2000.

The double cost of arms

In 1995, £13 billion of arms were sold to the developing world.[46] In poor countries with high military spending, very little money is available for health and education. As Somalia in the 1980s descended into increasing violence and worsening poverty, military spending was five times the combined budgets for health and education.

Since the end of the war in Ethiopia in 1991, the size of the army has been halved. Defence spending has fallen from US$610 million in 1985 to US$111 ten years later.[47] Social spending has simultaneously increased, and the same positive trend of falling military expenditure and rising social spending has been seen in the mid-1990s in Eritrea, Uganda, Mozambique, and Zimbabwe.[48] The impact can be seen in the lives of at least some of their people. Eritrea has built small dams and reservoirs, dug wells, prepared over 2,000 hectares of cropland and planted millions of trees.[49] An earlier positive example was provided by Costa Rica, which abolished its army in 1949, and as a result has been able to improve the living standards of its people with the resources it saved by avoiding heavy military spending.[50] This, and the fact that Cost Rica has been at peace, are among the reasons why Costa Rica is now number 33 on the list of countries of the world ranked according to development criteria; neighbouring El Salvador, Guatemala, and Nicaragua come around numbers 112 to 127 on that list.[51]

What poor countries spend on arms is very small compared to the budgets of richer countries. In 1995, the OECD countries still accounted for 75 per cent of global military expenditure. Africa south of the Sahara spent US$8.2 billion in 1995, the same year in which Britain spent four times as much (US$34 billion). In per capita terms, sub-Saharan Africa spent only US$20 a year, compared to Britain's US$586 and the NATO average of US$396. Yet the percentages of GDP spent on arms are very similar. Sub-Saharan Africa spends 2.8 per cent, Britain 3.1 per cent, and the NATO average is 2.5 per cent (while the arms-race regions of East Asia and the Middle East produce figures of 4.5 per cent and 6.5 per cent).[52] However, the tiny budgets of poor countries, and the huge social demands on them, mean that this level of military spending frequently has a serious impact on the ability of governments to provide essential services. In any country, rich or poor, the balance between military and social spending is crucial; while governments may have legitimate defence needs, to spend relatively more on the military than on health and education would surely call their priorities into question.

The UN Children's Fund estimates that everyone in the world could receive basic social services, such as health care, education, and safe water, at a cost of an additional US$40 billion a year above existing spending on those services. The governments of developing countries themselves could, if they wished, meet two-thirds of this cost by changing their own budget priorities including cutting military spending.[53] That is the logic behind the growing belief since the mid-1990s that a compact should be agreed between the governments of poor countries, and those of rich countries. The former should spend 20 per cent of their budgets, the latter 20 per cent of their aid, on priority social programmes. Though such an arrangement was endorsed by governments at the

World Summit on Social Development in Copenhagen in 1995, many governments have still made little or no progress in this direction.[54] But it would be an obvious way of reducing the double cost to the poorest and most vulnerable of excessive arms spending.

The next steps

The interest in landmines is an almost unprecedented example of public and political concern, across continents, for a remarkably cheap and basic weapon. Since the gas attacks of the First World War, chemical and biological weapons, and weapons of mass destruction, have dominated international interest. The proliferation of landmines, and small arms more generally, illustrates the way in which producer countries have helped to create the problem of modern war. Yet public opinion has succeeded in influencing governments in producer countries and others, to take steps to find a solution to this problem. At the beginning of January 1995, no government was committed to banning anti-personnel mines; within less than three years, nearly half the world's governments had agreed to do so. This and the other positive recent developments point to a future agenda for controlling small arms, and tackling their effects, ranging from the ethical regulation of the legal trade, a greater crack-down on the illegal market, and investing in 'buy-back' and demining as part of coherent reconstruction and development programmes in the countries affected. Chapter 7 will point to these in more detail. Before that, Chapter 4 will look at other aspects of the international response to conflict in the 1990s.

4 The international response to war

Before a war breaks out, there are a range of policy choices which the international community can make which have the effect of making conflict more or less likely. If economic reform policies had not helped to destroy the livelihood opportunities for tens of thousands of Rwandans from the late 1980s, the risk of genocide *might* have been smaller. If the leaders who plunged former Yugoslavia into war had been decisively warned in the early 1990s that they had no hope of international recognition or support if they pursued ethnically-divisive policies, the Balkans *might* have escaped the wars that followed. We will look at the risk factors and 'triggers' which tend to lead to armed conflict, and how these can be countered, in the next chapter.

Yet once a war has started, the options are both fewer and more hazardous. Most obviously, the 'last resort' option of UN-sanctioned force may be necessary in extreme cases, as Oxfam argued in Rwanda and former Zaire, and Bosnia; but it is never without great risks or inevitable suffering. The difficulty of responding to current wars does not remove the responsibility of the world's governments to do what they can to mediate, and to help the victims. What finally brought the conflicts in Bosnia, Haiti, and Mozambique to an end demonstrates both that there can be solutions, and that sometimes they involve action. This might include cutting the supply of arms and ammunition flowing into the war zones, but could also include a coherent message that all international contact will be conditional on the leaders' performance on human rights and a determined search for a peaceful resolution to the conflict. Besides these incentives of diplomatic and economic recognition, there could be the additional pressures of sanctions specifically targeted on political leaders' foreign bank accounts and travel, and determined efforts to bring war criminals to justice.

The actions required in each case are likely to be very different. Good practice in such 'peace-making' is still unclear because there are few examples of where the 'international community' has put a determined effort into helping to make that peace. This chapter will argue that too often the only substantial international response to current wars has been emergency relief — and that too little, too variable in its quality and, without the provision of protection for its recipients, often too compromised. This leaves millions of men, women, and children suffering in extreme circumstances in their homes or in neighbouring countries to which they have fled. The few who flee to Western countriesy have also tended to face a less hospitable welcome in the 1990s; the chapter will end by examining the shortcomings of asylum policies.

Aid as a 'fig leaf'

Humanitarian aid is essential both to save lives and provide for the basic needs of the most vulnerable people in wars. But to some extent, humanitarian aid has become a 'fig leaf' behind which governments can hide their failure to act to protect civilians in war, and to help to bring the war to an end, and prevent further wars. Médecins sans Frontières first used this colourful phrase in 1993,[1] but in 1996 the European Commission made the same attack in the same words at the Florence summit of the European Union. Aid policy has replaced foreign policy for countries where the major powers perceive little economic interest — or no immediate threat of refugees from wars in their 'backyards'.

Even in Bosnia, 'humanitarian aid [was] the solution to a problem caused by humanitarian aid'.[2] It is at least arguable that the war could have been resolved before most of its 200,000 victims died if European Union member states, and the United States, had decided on firm diplomatic and military measures at the outset.

Much has been written on the series of EU and UN diplomatic efforts which took place until the fall of Srebrenica in July 1995, and of the UN and various governments' dishonourable role. All these efforts failed either to end the war or to protect its victims. In the summer of 1995 a different strategy was adopted which proved successful.[3] One reason for the failure of the international effort from 1992, when the war moved to Bosnia after its referendum for independence, until 1995, was that the humanitarian operation was presented as the over-riding purpose of international intervention, which might be jeopardised by the use of force.

In most other wars of the 1990s, the energetic action represented by the Dayton negotiations, and the international commitment since then, have not even been considered. In 1996, the ground-breaking international evaluation, commissioned by OECD governments and others, of the response to Rwanda's genocide, characterised that response as a 'policy vacuum'. Despite warnings of a comprehensive design for systematic killings from, among others, the UN Commission on Human Rights, and the UN peace-keeping commander on the ground, the list of what could have happened, but did not, is long. Aid donors did not set strict human rights conditions on their aid, to send a firm message that they would not tolerate major violence. They did not offer sufficient support to the Organisation of African Unity as it struggled to implement the 1993 Arusha Accords. And the UN Security Council sent a peace-keeping mission, with a weak mandate and little capacity to, for example, seize the arms caches which were being built up with supplies from France and other countries.

In June 1997, the authors of the international evaluation of emergency assistance to Rwanda, published 15 months earlier, produced a review of follow-up and impact,[4] which asked how much had been learnt from the failure of policies and the inaction of 1994: 'The critical bottom-line question has to be, could the events of 1994 happen again?' While they observed that progress had been made by many organisations, including the World Bank, UNHCR, and aid donors, they saw little change in the working of the UN Security Council in terms of improving transparency and consistency. The contrast between its comparative energy on Albania in 1997, and lack of energy in former Zaire, seemed stark. They concluded:

In Burundi over the past year ... the international mechanisms and willingness to prevent extraordinary levels of violence and massive human rights abuses have been tragically deficient... alongside the lack of progress on the issues of policy coherence and genocide prevention, the case of Burundi must lead us to conclude that, one year on, a great deal has not changed, despite all the debate...[5]

The world is no longer divided by the ideological battle field of the Cold War, but other divisions remain, which help to decide which wars do, and which do not, receive attention from the international community.

Two worlds

When George Bush left the White House in January 1993, it already seemed that his earlier vision of a 'new world order', after the Cold War, had been optimistic. Though the recent arrival of US troops in Somalia had not yet descended into the disasters they faced later that year, the world seemed a more, not less, violent place. The then British Foreign Secretary, Douglas Hurd, dubbed the decade, more pessimistically, the 'new world disorder'.

Most wars from the 1950s to the 1980s, almost 200 in number,[6] had taken place in the 'developing world' and many of them had been 'proxy wars' supported by the Soviet Union or the United States. In the past, the poorer countries of the world had been referred to successively as colonies, developing countries, the Third World, and the South. Nowadays, these terms all seem redundant, as significant parts of the South have become dynamic economic regions: South-East Asia, South Africa, and the Mercosur countries of Latin America. In parallel, some former Soviet-bloc countries have seen rapidly falling living standards.

The world at the end of the twentieth century is divided into 'insider' regions of comparative prosperity and security, where economic growth combines with increasing regional economic integration, and 'outsider' regions of growing poverty and conflict, where the nation state is not sharing its power in wider regional organisations, but more often collapsing, with wars fought over demands for separation by one ethnic group or local area or another. Typically, the 'outsiders' are becoming poorer, with weak economies and little capacity to export goods for profit. The economies of a hundred countries are not growing, but declining or stagnating, reducing the incomes of 1.6 billion people, a quarter of the world's population.[7] Their governments are often burdened by debt. The only dynamic parts of some economies may be the illicit extraction of raw materials by warlords linked to foreign investors.

In a world in which foreign policy is no longer based on Cold War geopolitics, but on geo-economics, this divide between those who participate successfully in the global economy and those who are excluded also largely defines which wars are deemed serious problems by Western governments, and which are not. The 'insider' regions straddle the old North-South divide: the EU and the countries of Central and Eastern Europe seeking membership; the Mediterranean countries negotiating a free trade area with the EU; members of the North American Free Trade Agreement and the Mercosur in Latin America; the Gulf oil states; South Africa; and the Pacific rim countries of the Asia and Pacific Economic Community.[8] But most of Africa, and some of Asia, is off the map.

This broad-brush picture is not intended to hide the very real differences between countries in the same region. There is also growing inequality within many countries, including the 'South' within the 'North'.[9] The distribution of benefits within the globalised economy is extremely skewed, with some regions and groups that lack access to skills and capital becoming increasingly marginalised.

'Insider' and 'outsider' wars

Where recent wars have taken place in economically important areas, many have been resolved, and refugees from them are returning; though not, as in former Yugoslavia, always to the place where they had previously lived, and the wrongs of the wars may not have been righted. This is not to suggest that conflicts which take place in countries where there is major foreign investment are without immense suffering — or easy to resolve. But that *most* such wars are eventually resolved seems, at least in part, due to outside powers seeing their interests threatened by the continued bloodshed. By the late 1980s, apartheid had become an economic problem to the West, and sanctions gave the South African government the increasingly clear message that its policies were no longer tolerable. By 1995, the conflict in Bosnia, and the cost to the West's credibility from its continuance, had also become intolerable. After three years of war, and the murder of perhaps 7,000 in Srebrenica that July, NATO's air strikes, and assertive American diplomacy, gave the Serb government and its Bosnian clients the clearest possible message that the war must end.

Both conflicts[10] were being fought in places that 'mattered'. Their economic importance, or their proximity to Western Europe — which was unwilling to accept more refugees — meant that their conflicts had to be stopped. This demonstrated what the Gulf War showed even more starkly in 1990-91: that immediate threats to the interests of the major Western powers provoke political energy and unblock resources — in a way that threats to the values of human rights have seldom done.

The 1990s have seen major powers in most continents help to end wars. In May 1994, for example, the war between Abkhazia and Georgia was suspended by the Moscow Agreement when Russia decided that peace in its 'sphere of influence' was preferable to its previous support for the Abkhazian separatists. In the case of Haiti, which sits in the United States' 'backyard', US pressure in 1994 eventually helped to remove the junta which had ousted the elected President Aristide three years earlier. The restored government was then protected by the pressure of 22,000 soldiers, all but a thousand of whom were from the US.[11] In 1997, South Africa's attempts to bring a peaceful transition of power in former Zaire may well be seen as a turning point in its influence across the continent.

In stark contrast, when wars occur in the world 'outside' the global economy, emergency aid often remains the only major response by Western governments to these distant 'unimportant' wars, which do not immediately threaten important economic interests. When images from them appear on television screens, branded emergency aid successfully demonstrates that Western governments are 'taking action'.

Humanitarian aid

Spending on humanitarian relief rose sharply in the early 1990s but appears to have peaked at US$6 billion in 1994.[12] It fell to around US$4.2 billion in 1995, and most major donors suggest that their 1997 spending will continue this decline.[13] Though the wars of the early 1990s forced up the proportion of official aid which went on emergencies to 9 per cent,[14] the trend now seems to be in reverse; in 1995, the proportion was down again to 7 per cent.[15] Britain's bilateral emergency aid peaked at £209 million in 1994-95, and then fell to £142 million in 1995-96.[16] The EU's budget for emergency aid fell from 764 million ecu in 1994, to 692 million in 1995 and only 657 million in 1996. Indeed, by the end of 1996 only 340 million ecu had been issued in contracts out of this reduced budget, compared to 680 million in 1995. Though more funds from the 1996 budget would be released in 1997, the amount of EU money actually spent on emergencies seems to be falling even faster than the official decline in the amounts budgeted.[17]

More importantly, the humanitarian aid provided is almost never adequate for the people who need it, either in conflicts (which account for 80 per cent of emergency aid) or natural disasters. Since 1992, the United Nations has issued Consolidated Appeals for major emergencies, most of them caused by wars, hoping to raise funds from 'donor governments'. While they received 79 per cent of their budgets in 1994, it was 71 per cent in 1995, and down to 65 per cent in 1996.[18] Comparatively generous donations tend to flow to emergencies in the media spotlight: virtually 100 per cent for former Yugoslavia from 1993 to 1995, though falling to 69 per cent while the area was comparatively out of the news, in 1996. Other crises, with perhaps just as much human need, are largely ignored. In 1996, donors covered only 51 per cent of the UN appeal for Sudan, 48 per cent for the Caucasus, and just 20 per cent for Somalia.[19] This bias in funding UN appeals seems to be generally true of most official emergency aid. In 1994, the main donor governments gave US$289 a head in aid to former Yugoslavia, while Afghanistan received only US$37, Liberia US$25, and Ethiopia US$17 per head, respectively.[20]

It seems that the world's attention can only cope with one major emergency at a time. What chance have people suffering in emergencies which are not in the media spotlight? The first head of the UN's Department of Humanitarian Affairs, the respected Swedish diplomat Jan Eliasson, pondered sadly that a child in any war is more likely to survive if he or she appears on CNN.[21]

Aid and the abuse of aid [22]

In the late 1990s, the future of humanitarian aid is now perhaps more in question than at any time since 1945. The providers ask whether the abuse of aid outweighs its benefits. The donors, at least the official ones, are reducing their funding. Yet the need for aid continues. In May 1997, a new record may have been reached, as 300 per 10,000 people were dying every day in Kisangani in former Zaire.[23] Although fewer people worldwide were in need of aid in 1997 than in the previous year, the estimated figure of 36.2 million remained three times as high as the numbers in the early 1980s.[24]

Adam Roberts, Professor of International Relations at Oxford University, is critical of the lack of protection given to the victims of war, but judges that recent aid has saved many lives:

Humanitarian efforts ... averted the worst consequences of famine in Somalia in 1992-93. It subsequently prevented or mitigated at least two widely predicted disasters — mass starvation in Sarajevo in the three winters starting in 1992-93, and the uncontrolled spread of the extensive outbreaks of cholera and dysentery in the camps on the borders of Rwanda in 1994.[25]

If fighters are taking some of the aid, and perhaps selling it to buy guns, there comes a time when donor governments and humanitarian agencies must ask themselves whether that aid is doing more harm than good. Humanitarian aid certainly *can* prolong wars, and so cause more human suffering than it is meant to relieve. One example of this was when the factional fighting in the Liberian capital of Monrovia escalated in April 1996. The subsequent looting by warlords of more than 400 aid vehicles and millions of dollars of equipment and relief goods led several NGOs to agree to minimise their assistance to Liberia until guarantees to respect the right of people }to humanitarian assistance were forthcoming. The looting had not only prevented aid reaching civilians in need, but also contributed materially to the war as vehicles and radio equipment were used for military purposes.

Twelve international NGOs therefore decided to limit their work, using locally available equipment, with no new resources going into Liberia which could fuel its 'war economy'. However, the NGOs still sought to respond where the lack of aid would have threatened people's lives. Consequently, in September 1996 in response to new evidence of starvation, Oxfam set up a feeding programme[26] which sought to meet urgent needs at the same time as keeping to the principle of 'minimum inputs' (of lootable goods) for 'maximum impact' (for the vulnerable population). So-called 'smart' aid to Liberia not only puts in the least level of capital goods in order to lessen the temptation to looting; it also emphasises the right of civilians to be protected from violence and supports the development of impartial civilian organisations.

In other wars too, there are strategies, more or less planned, to divert aid both to reward fighters and to keep the war going. When the *genocidaires* of Rwanda's former army, militia, and extremist political parties were routed from some of the camps in eastern Zaire in November 1996, they left behind them documents confirming that *Operation Insecticide*, the plan to complete the genocide through terrorism and re-invading Rwanda, was well advanced — whether realistic or not. That *Operation*, had it been carried out, would have been partly sustained by the international aid provided by Oxfam and others to the 1.2 million refugees controlled, until then, by the *genocidaire* leaders.

In Somalia in the early 1990s, the rents and payments to the so-called 'technicals' — the package of Landrover and armed guards which aid agencies bought[27] — provided hard currency for arms, while the factions fought over food aid and water points.

Tough choices

When some aid is misappropriated, the question arises whether the net impact of the aid is positive or negative? Is the greatest threat to life the lack of food and other necessities, which aid can relieve; or the violence which may directly or indirectly result from the abuse of that aid? Looted aid is often sold to buy extra weapons to be used some time later. The threat of starvation or death from disease must be real and demonstrable to justify giving aid, some of which is likely to be diverted.

In all such cases, the providers of aid have to make the acutely difficult judgement on whether the net impact of their work adds to or diminishes the total of human suffering. Meeting the need for material relief is no longer an over-riding objective, but one that must be balanced against the harm which may come from abuse of that relief.

49

The real victims of wars are not helped by looking at the question of net impact from either of two extremes: the view that 'human rights', narrowly defined as civil and political rights, are superior to the rights, equally present in international law, to humanitarian aid (i.e. to food, water, and shelter); nor the view that what used to be called the 'humanitarian imperative' to deliver aid outweighs any negative side-effects. The term used to describe the situations in many countries currently at war is 'complex emergencies'. They certainly produce ethical complexities.

Beyond these obvious ethical dilemmas, there are a host of others which have arisen in many current wars. Does providing humanitarian aid in conflict areas indirectly allow a government to spend resources on fighting a war, which would otherwise have been spent on the provision of services? Can aid agencies reach those who are in most need, or only those whom the combatants allow them to? In 1997 in central Africa, agencies have not had access to hundreds of thousands of victims of the region's wars. When David Bryer, Director of Oxfam, addressed members of the UN Security Council in February 1997, he said that the agency had contingency stocks in Burundi sufficient for 200,000 people, but they could do only limited good because the level of insecurity and the attitude of the authorities prevented Oxfam getting access to people in urgent need. Burundi's authorities had 'regrouped' people into camps, ostensibly for their safety, but apparently also as a tactic to flush out rebels. The question of whether to 'collude' by giving aid in the camps, or to refuse to co-operate with the authorities, thus denying people relief, has challenged aid agencies throughout 1997. In neighbouring former Zaire, in April of that year, agencies helping refugees coming out of the forest on their way to Bukavu feared that they were being used to lure people to where many were killed by the rebel Alliance des Forces Democratiques pour la Liberation de Congo. On the Rwandan side of the border, Oxfam had had to leave Kibuye in early February because of the worsening war, though only after it had been able to set up a water supply for 12,000. As Bryer told the Security Council, the worst irony is that: 'Where access is most difficult is likely to be where the human needs are most acute.'[28]

When agencies threaten to stop work in a country because of abuses of human rights, this can sometimes put pressure on the authorities to change their behaviour. In 1989, Oxfam suspended its relief operations in the Kumi region of Uganda in protest at the government's counter-insurgency campaign, and in that instance the government policy was changed.[29]

Armed aid

As Oxfam has worked alongside several peace-keeping operations in the 1990s, it has had a greater contact with the military than ever before. Though the military capacity for very rapid air-lifts can sometimes be vital in the first days of an emergency, the advantage soon wears off, and becomes outweighed by the typically very high costs. The 1996 Rwanda evaluation calculated that military aircraft cost typically between four and eight times as much as hiring civil contractors.[30]

In cases where the delivery of aid itself demands the skills of military pilots, they should be used. Flying into besieged cities may often involve the kind of dramatic descents and take-offs practised by the air force pilots of UNHCR's long airlift to Sarajevo. But this is not the norm.

When it is impossible to work without the protection of UN peace-keepers or others, are the benefits outweighed by the disadvantages? With such UN military protection, aid agencies lose much of their image of impartiality — and therefore become more vulnerable to attack by at least one side. In Somalia, this was hardly surprising given the partial actions of UNOSOM. But even in Bosnia, where UNPROFOR could perhaps be criticised for being *too* neutral, it and nearly all the aid agencies were perceived at times as partisan. In fact, each party to the war sought to manipulate humanitarian aid for its own ends.

Aid agencies differ on the merits of accepting UN protection. The Red Cross does not accept armed protection, seeing this as a threat to its neutrality. Other agencies, on occasion, do. But whether or not military protection actually puts aid workers at greater risk, it is certain that providing aid has become a far more dangerous[31] occupation in recent years. The question arises whether working in wars is now putting aid workers at unacceptable risk.

Conditional aid

To Oxfam's founders during the Second World War, it was of crucial significance that civilians in the occupied countries of Nazi Europe should not be held responsible for the crimes of their oppressors. The Oxford Committee for Famine Relief was set up as one of a network of campaigning groups around the country trying to persuade the British government to lift the Allied blockade, to let aid through to civilians dying of starvation in occupied Greece.

The rights of individuals in wars are not unconditional, either legally or morally: the 1951 Refugee Convention excludes from its protection those guilty of serious crimes against humanity. There is no obligation to provide relief for those who have committed grave abuses of human rights. The immunity which the Geneva Conventions provides to civilians is given precisely on the condition that they are not fighting.

For this reason, many NGOs sought from 1994 to persuade Zaire and the 'international community' to separate the genuine Rwandan refugees in eastern Zaire from the minority among them suspected of participating in the genocide. That the call went unheeded left hundreds of thousands of refugees as virtual captives of the extremists until the action of Tutsi rebels at the end of 1996.

In southern Sudan, NGOs have been closely observing how the UN Children's Fund and the Sudan People's Liberation Movement have agreed so-called 'ground rules' to protect both aid and civilians from some of the worst ravages of the long-running war. Based on the Geneva Conventions and the 1989 Convention on the Rights of the Child, the rules, in essence, state that aid will only go through the SPLM's relief arm if the fighters meet the condition of upholding relevant international law. The 1996 review of Operation Lifeline Sudan described it as a model for ethical behaviour in other wars. However, some aid agencies have feared that the practice has not been as effective as the theory. It is perhaps obvious that at times of high military tension, combatants are less willing to abide by the rules. The rules agreed in this case seem to have had some effect in making fighters more conscious of the rights of civilians to protection, and perhaps more aware that it is unacceptable for aid to be diverted for military purposes.

Humanitarian standards

Some agencies are showing a greater awareness of the net impact of their work, and a greater commitment to transparent self-regulation of the 'humanitarian industry'. Though media criticisms of NGOs are not always just, their work should always be open to critical evaluation and consequent improvement. Unless an agency can demonstrate that the net impact of its work is positive, it does not deserve support.

The competition for funds between relief agencies — UN agencies and others — and the competition for profile by NGOs and donor governments may be understandable. All of them need media coverage to attract further donations, or to justify to their electorates that they are spending public funds effectively. Yet competition can sometimes descend, as it did among some agencies in former Zaire, to an unseemly jostle to be seen, with little heed given to the need to co-operate, or to provide the best service for the refugees. This calls into question the legitimacy and value to beneficiaries of the work of such agencies; eventually, it reduces the respect in which all aid agencies are held, and makes it less likely that they will be able to help the victims of future emergencies. Improving the situation depends not only on a more co-operative operational approach among agencies, but also on more honest fundraising, which several British agencies have sought to foster through a joint code of conduct.

Another way in which a number of NGOs are seeking to improve their response is through the agreement of minimum standards for the provision of shelter, food, water, and health care. The Steering Committee for Humanitarian Response (SCHR) is the main international network of relief agencies.[32] Together, these agencies deliver most of the world's emergency aid handled by voluntary organisations. In 1994, SCHR agreed a *Code of Conduct for Disaster Relief*.

Putting into effect the Code's general principles, all these agencies are now working with the US network InterAction and others, and governments, to agree minimum standards, setting out with some precision what every civilian in any emergency has a right to, and therefore what humanitarian agencies and donor governments have a responsibility to provide. It is right that aid agencies should seek to be more accountable both to their donors and to the people whom they are meant to serve. The development of these standards is an important step towards greater accountability.

Reforming the UN system

If the performance of voluntary aid agencies has been variable, the same is true of the official relief operations of different branches of the UN. The co-ordination among the cluster of UN agencies with some humanitarian functions has frequently been poor, marred by 'turf battles' and, as among NGOs, intense competition for funds. Following much criticism of the way in which aid was delivered to the Iraqi Kurds in 1991, a UN Department of Humanitarian Affairs was established with the purpose, though without the authority, to deliver a more coherent approach.

The new UN Secretary-General, Kofi Annan, proposed modest changes in July 1997, effectively renaming the DHA's core as the Office of the Emergency Relief Co-ordinator. How this works out in practice will be crucially important for millions of women, men, and children caught up in wars (and natural disasters). As well as ensuring better co-ordination, the slightly modified system will need to increase the protection to those who are 'internally displaced', but not formal refugees, as well as focus more strongly on the protection of refugees, rather than just relief provision. Although in practice, UNHCR increasingly considers internally displaced people as legitimate targets for its concern, officially they are outside UNHCR's current mandate, and therefore more vulnerable.

The plight of refugees

Support for refugees has been declining in recent years. UNHCR states that in the post-Cold-War 1990s, there is less and less a 'strategic interest in refugees'[33] driving governments' generosity. Vietnamese 'boat people' are no longer seen as a useful embarrassment for Hanoi; Nicaraguan *contras*, Afghan *mujahideen*, or some Angolan refugees in Namibia, are no longer useful 'warrior refugees' to train, supply, and send back to fight Communism.

The result is not only diminishing international support for refugees, and the neighbouring governments and communities hosting them, but also a less hospitable climate for the few who do manage to travel further. This is partly because the numbers arriving as asylum-seekers in most industrialised countries grew very significantly in the late 1980s and early 1990s. The numbers applying in Britain peaked in 1991 at 44,840, slightly more than ten times the figure in 1985.[34] But by 1996, they were down to 27,930.[35]

The numbers accepted have also increased compared to the 1980s — but not at the same rate as applications. In 1994, a quarter of a million people obtained asylum or protection in the industrialised world, compared to 136,000 in 1985.[36] Across Western Europe, applications more than trebled over the same ten years to 318,887 by 1994, largely because of the wars in former Yugoslavia.[37] Western governments, often appeasing what they perceive as increasingly intolerant public opinion, have treated applicants with great harshness. This leaves the individual, 'effectively presumed "bogus" unless and until he or she can prove beyond reasonable (and sometimes unreasonable) doubt that his or her fear of persecution is well-founded'.[38]

Western European countries as a whole have done more to avoid than to share the burden of taking in those seeking refuge from wars and persecution. Various EU decisions have placed the responsibility on the country of 'first safe arrival' to judge asylum applications, though it is frequently debatable which that country is. Is an airport transit lounge a 'first arrival'? Is France 'safe' for refugees from France's sometimes dictatorial allies in Africa? Such arguments often result in long delays and in applicants 'being bounced back and forth like ping-pong balls between different European countries'.[39]

Growing intolerance

The intolerant minority are increasingly vocal in many European countries. Their view is articulated in a language reminiscent of the hatreds from civil wars around the world, of uncompromising attacks upon the 'other'. In February 1997, the National Front candidate in the southern French town of Vitrolles, Catherine Megret, explaining her election victory, said: 'Our voters wanted us to scare people who don't belong.'[40]

One explanation for increasing intolerance and more restrictive policies in the West is the fear of unemployment:

By the late 1980s ... high unemployment rates, the increased numbers of immigrants, and their overwhelmingly 'non-European' character produced sharp changes in European attitudes and policies. A few years later similar concerns led to a comparable shift in the United States.[41]

Unemployment perhaps more than anything else helps to create a climate conducive to extremist and racist intolerance. To Jean-Marie le Pen, 'two million immigrants, two million unemployed' has been an effective political slogan. In Britain, asylum-seekers have been portrayed as social security 'scroungers' by some parts of the media and by the previous UK government.

Changing policy in the UK

In 1996, only 6 per cent of applicants were granted asylum in Britain.[42] But was this really because 94 per cent were 'bogus'? The fact that in Canada, for example, the proportion of successful applicants rose sharply after the process was reformed, could lead to the 'uncomfortably plausible' explanation of Britain's very low rate of acceptance as being because Britain's process is so unfair.[43]

Britain has also been among those countries which have used detention and restrictions in social security apparently as a means to convince potential asylum-seekers that they would be better off not coming to the country at all. The MP Alan Howarth, who left the Conservatives for Labour in 1996, put this level of intolerance in historical proportion:

For the first time in our history [the previous British Government] has deliberately, and indeed unlawfully, acted to leave families destitute.[44]

Oxfam supports a range of projects with asylum-seekers and refugees, as part of its increased focus on poverty in Britain. One is the British Refugee Council's Karibu Centre in London, which provides food and other necessities to refugees who are not able to claim social security. Cali, from Colombia, visits the Centre. She arrived in Britain at the end of 1996. In Colombia, she owned a small business, and had a knowledge of banking, so she was seized by guerillas who wanted her to help them defraud banks:

When I refused to help them, they tortured me. They beat me so badly that I now have a bad back and my breasts are permanently scarred. My husband was tortured as well. Eventually we pretended to co-operate and had to swear loyalty to the group. Then we ran away and eventually got out of the country and came to England.

We tried to seek asylum when we arrived at the airport, but the immigration officer wasn't very sympathetic. He finally let us come into the country as tourists on a temporary visa, but he wouldn't acknowledge us as asylum-seekers so we are not allowed to claim benefits. He just laughed when we said we wanted to seek asylum...[45]

Conflict — to contain or to resolve?

Other Western European governments have taken similar measures to Britain's, and sometimes more restrictive ones. The German government, too, has cut benefits to asylum seekers. In 1993, the French government made it more difficult for the children of foreigners to acquire citizenship, for families of foreigners to take up residence in France, and for Algerians to get visas to cross the Mediterranean.[46] In early 1997, a bill going further, including allowing the authorities to fingerprint non-Europeans seeking residence, brought 100,000 protestors on to the streets of Paris.[47] And in the US, the Clinton Administration ended three decades of policy granting asylum to Cubans.[48]

If the increasing reluctance to accept refugees were because governments were putting their energies into preventing wars starting in the first place, this could be seen as reasonable: dealing with the cause of the problem is better than treating the symptom of refugees turning up in Europe. Of course, the policies should not be seen as alternatives. But the annual cost of US$10 billion to pay for Western asylum systems should surely act as a major incentive for those governments to invest effectively to reduce the human suffering from which refugees hope to escape.[49]

Unfortunately, not only is the treatment of refugees expensively inhumane, but most Western governments have put a low emphasis on protecting them in their countries of origin, or on the prevention of war. The purpose of policy:

... is shifting towards the containment of refugees, rather than their protection. When containment fails, and the refugees make it to the country of asylum, the emphasis is placed on removing them as soon as possible.[50]

Global responsibility

Throughout, this book has argued that the prime responsibility for the violence in modern wars, as well as the prime hope for solutions, lies in the countries in, or on the edge of war. But the failure of international diplomacy described above is also important. It signifies the decline of what used to be called 'internationalism' and the failure to present this afresh in a way which can connect to the ideas of the 1990s and beyond. Internationalism is not a new idea; one of its great proponents this century between the two world wars was Gilbert Murray, later to become one of the founders of Oxfam. Sometimes known as 'universalism' (or 'interdependence', Willy Brandt's name for it in the 1980s), it is simply the belief that each person has a global responsibility — a responsibility to others around the world, beyond direct or short-term self-interest. Under whatever name, it has always been a combination of enlightened self-interest, a moral anger at injustice, and a solidarity with people in need of help.

The growing inequality between people and countries in the globalised economy is a major threat to internationalism. The lack of concern about people in countries where there is little economic interest is foreign policy driven by short-term geo-economics. Particularly in the United States, this has been described as a new isolationism — a term applied to previous periods of American foreign policy which, as today, have managed to combine efforts for economic expansion, with declining responsibility for anything beyond that.[51]

The same trend is becoming noticeable in Europe. Yet in a world where inequality, social exclusion, and the suffering in wars is increasing, internationalism has never been more relevant. Chapter 7 suggests what it could mean in practice: international arms control; a more assertive attempt to bring war criminals to justice; a UN Security Council more transparent and determined to send firm signals to leaders who incite violence; humanitarian aid judged against accepted standards and its 'net impact'; and fairer treatment of refugees and asylum seekers.

To return to the point with which this chapter started: preventing wars is both cheaper and less hazardous than resolving them once they have begun. For this reason, the most important aspect of a revived internationalism would be to do more to reduce the risks of future wars, the subject of the next chapter.

5 Reducing the risks of war

War can not always be prevented; that is why international support for the protection of civilians during wars is essential. But although it may not be possible to avoid violent conflict in all cases, there are certain factors which tend to increase the *risk* of war, which could be addressed in order to reduce that risk. Governments, international organisations, companies — and aid agencies — should test all their policies for their effect on increasing or reducing violations of human rights and the risk of war. Environmental-impact assessments have helped to improve awareness, and change policies; it is now time to introduce 'conflict-impact assessments'.

Sometimes, seeking to reduce armed conflicts may produce tough choices: for example, to target aid to an unstable country when another is poorer. But the conditions which increase the risks of war are evils in themselves which need to be remedied: gross inequality, a weak and corrupt government, and the denial of people's basic rights. When large numbers of citizens experience social, political, and economic exclusion war becomes more likely.

As well as this range of risk factors, governments and others should also be aware of the 'triggers' — often the actions of ruthless leaders — which turn an unstable situation into a war.

War and exclusion

There is no single explanation for any particular war. Nor can war be prevented simply by good governance or better development aid. But even the application of common sense on what is likely to increase the risks of violence could have a major benefit. Margaret Anstee, the British former head of the UN mission in Angola, said in February 1997 that there were just some 'blinding glimpses of the obvious' to throw light on what tended to cause conflicts and what could help to resolve them.[1]

But it can be obvious and still not be acted on. For example, it seems likely that when people are desperately poor, they are more ready to believe propaganda that some other social group is to blame for their suffering, and to join armed factions who promise redress for their wrongs. It may be obvious, but Western governments still spend a very small proportion of their aid on tackling poverty rather than on prestige projects. In 1995, 4 per cent of official aid from the OECD countries went to provide clean water and sanitation, 0.3 per cent on primary health care, and only 0.1 per cent on the basic investments in learning: primary schools and literacy.[2] War is more likely to happen when there are no peaceful ways to climb out of poverty. What makes for a secure society is not so much an impartial civil police, but a successful and equitable economy and an inclusive politics in which everyone feels they have a stake.

But not every poor country in the world is at war; some grossly unequal societies are, if not exactly at peace, at least free from major armed conflict. And yet it can not be coincidence that most wars *are* fought in countries which are poor, divided by differences in wealth and identity, and where the political and legal systems are weak and can not facilitate peaceful change.

It seems clear that some of the factors which increase the risks of civil war, and make societies less stable are:

- deep ethnic or religious divisions — particularly if people see that they suffer because of their group identity, and blame another group for this;
- intense inequality and competition over the means to earn a living — particularly if both are rapidly increasing;
- no democratic rule of law or institutional framework to allow peaceful change or a regulated market economy;
- a ready supply of small arms and ammunition.

Something which has become more obvious in the 1990s is that violence does not happen without a cause: it is in someone's interest. Perhaps invariably, wars begin because individual leaders, and political elites, see some advantage to them in armed violence. Yet for leaders to be supported by thousands of people who take up arms, requires those people to make the same calculation. The question is: what so dramatically limits their choices to make this a rational option?

People are more likely to resort to violence if they have a grievance which can be shared with others by seeing it as a noble struggle for identity. People are more likely to fight if they are desperate. People are more likely to fight if they can not get what they want, or need, by any other means. And people are able to fight most lethally if they can use an AK47 rather than a spear. Where all four of these are in place, a society is likely to be in trouble.

If people do not have a stake in a peaceful society, some may find one in war. If people have the opportunity to earn their living, receive decent services, have some say in their future — they have a stake in maintaining a society which meets their own needs. If people believe that society does not give them a fair share of its wealth, however little; if they do not receive fair treatment before the law, and have no influence on their society's policies, they may have little incentive in keeping the peace.

We will now look in more detail at some of the underlying factors which make war more likely, and how these might be addressed.

Ethnicity and nationalism

Most of the wars of the 1990s have been simplistically ascribed to ethnic and religious contests. In the Balkans, the Caucasus, Sri Lanka, in central and west Africa, the brutal wars of this decade have often been described as inevitable conflagrations between age-old ethnic enemies. Perhaps in all these cases, ethnicity has not 'caused' war, in that existing deep divisions would probably not have erupted into major violence if they had not been manipulated by ruthless leaders keen to gain or maintain power. And all these countries faced other problems which increased the risk of war. In reality, different risks merge together; as Oxfam's Emergencies Director observed in Burundi in 1995: 'There is little substantive difference between a description of Burundi as a country in the grip of a peasant uprising, and a country racked by ethnic conflict.' Yet there can be no doubt that strong ethnic identities, when defined by hatred of others, is one risk which must be tackled to avoid war.[3]

The evidence that ethnicity is one major factor increasing the risk of war is very strong. In some 70 countries in the 1990s particular groups have been seeking more political autonomy on ethnic grounds.[4] In many of these, tensions have increased. In some of them, major wars have broken out, in which the main strategic purpose seems to be to 'cleanse' a territory of another ethnic group. It is tragically ironic that much of this inter-ethnic violence has been based on differences which are terribly real to the killers, but have no basis in historical or anthropological reality. As Oxfam's representative in Rwanda at the time of the genocide, put it: 'However specious the arguments on which it is based, playing the ethnic card has succeeded.'[5]

There has been a decline in the extent to which people in several parts of the world identify with their once multicultural state. Though nostalgia for the Soviet Union is still widespread, millions who readily identified with *homus sovieticus* up to the 1980s, no longer do so. Now they are far more likely to describe themselves as Latvian, Abkhazian or Chechnyan. The converse is also true. The success of the still tentative but remarkable building of a new South Africa depends fundamentally upon more people identifying themselves as firstly South African, and only secondly as, for example, Afrikaner or Zulu. In a very real sense, peace in some societies rests on whether the civic or national identity wins over the ethnic or local.

There is a need to understand the past as well as the present in a way which can include all people. The hope for Rwanda remains the same as it was in December 1993, four months before the genocide began, when Oxfam's former representative there wrote:

In the end it will be essential to work out a truly national and non-sectarian interpretation of Rwanda's past, if the current wounds of ethnic conflict are to be healed.[6]

That may appear well-nigh impossible so soon after the 1994 genocide; but it is no less necessary. In former Yugoslavia, the Middle East, the Caucasus, perhaps in every conflict, narrow visions of history, going back in some cases to biblical times, still excuse terrible abuses on the grounds that past wrongs are being righted.

Self-determination

As well as being an alternative to dangerous exclusion, the politics of inclusion can also be seen as an alternative to the traditional notion of 'self-determination'. In the era of decolonisation, it was almost automatically equated with the pursuit of independent statehood. More recently, 'self-determination' has been invoked to justify many armed conflicts, including those seeking to redraw the often arbitrary borders bequeathed by colonialism. It may be too sweeping to assume that there should be no further new states created, or that partition is *never* a solution, but the general principle must surely be to pursue political and economic inclusion within existing states. It is the existence of economic, cultural, and legal discrimination, in the absence of inclusive politics, which fosters violent struggles for independent statehood.

Identity politics

Ethnic, national, or ideological identity is an almost universal element in 1990s politics. In itself, identity politics is morally neutral. It can be based on inclusion or on exclusion, on Mandela's attempts to include all South Africans in a new identity, or on the former Rwandan government's exclusion of the Tutsi refugees in Uganda. Ethnic identity can be a powerful cohesive force in resisting oppression, as in Colombia's 'communities of peace' mentioned in chapter 6.

The assertion of exclusive ethnic or religious identities can increase the risk of violence, particularly if identity is defined either by a sense of being victor or victim. But there is a further 'trigger' required to increase hatred between different groups to the level where people will kill each other by the thousand.

One explanation would be that such hatreds tend to combine with other trends, such as increasing inequality, to drive people to desperation. But there is also a more specific factor: individual political leaders. They can make things better — or much worse: 'bad leaders are usually the catalysts that turn potentially volatile situations into open warfare'.[7]

Leaders who calculate that war is in their interest may exploit feelings of ethnic tension or economic exclusion. This is not to diminish the responsibility of every person who commits atrocities in war. But even quite intense communal hatreds may not have led to war if they had not been fanned further by leaders with an interest in doing so. The brutal war in Liberia, which has killed at least 150,000 people[8] this decade, is 'tribal conflict by design', as Oxfam's Emergencies Coordinator there described it in 1996.[9] From Inkhatha in South Africa, to the Hindu BJP in India, and Russia's changing alliances between its ultra-nationalists and communists — the interests of some political leaders in increasing tensions which already exist are very clear.

In former Yugoslavia, in Rwanda before the 1994 genocide, and in *apartheid* South Africa, this stirring up of hostile identities was done primarily by the existing governments, in all these cases as strategies to maintain power threatened by, respectively, the fall of Communism, the Arusha accords, and the mounting condemnation of white rule.

In other cases, it has been opposition groups who have based their power on an existing rivalry, which they have then managed to inflame. African Rights has documented how 'exemplary terror' has been used deliberately and effectively by fighters from Mozambique to Liberia to increase ethnic discord and instability.[10] A firm stance against abuses of human rights, particularly to protect ethnic minorities, on the part of the international community, can be a vital pressure on 'bad leaders' on the verge of war. It is also essential that war criminals are held to account once the fighting has stopped.

Impunity or justice?

Genocide in Rwanda came at the end of 35 years of intermittent mass killings, which had never been properly punished. The impunity which two generations of killers had enjoyed may have encouraged those who planned and carried out the far larger massacres in 1994 to believe that they would never face justice. The international evaluation published in 1996 condemned this 'culture of impunity' as one factor which led to the most extreme violence. For any hope of a sustainable peace in the future, those who led the genocide must be brought to justice. Uwambeyi Esperance's husband and baby were killed in April 1994. A former civil servant, she survived terrible personal experiences during the genocide, and with other widows, has now formed an association for mutual support and counselling. Three years later, she says:

I feel that justice should be done so that other people should not have similar experiences. Those who did these things should be punished for what they have done ... To us victims it seems as though nothing is being done. We see people walking around who did things to us and we don't even know if anything is going to be done to them.[11]

Impunity for past atrocities not only suggests to extremists that their crimes will go unpunished. It may also make those who have been wronged live for the day when they can have their revenge. If people who have suffered do not see the individuals responsible being brought to justice, they are more likely to demonise whole groups: Hutu or Tutsi, Croats or Serbs. As President Clinton said in October 1995, shortly before peace was agreed at Dayton:

Those accused of war crimes, crimes against humanity and genocide must be brought to justice. They must be tried and if found guilty, they must be held accountable... There must be peace for justice to prevail. But there must be justice when peace prevails.[12]

In Bosnia, this has been the assumption behind the efforts to try war crimes suspects, and the seizure of suspects by NATO troops in June and July 1997.

Yet such an approach can be seen as directly at odds with the 'politics of inclusion' and reconciliation which also appears to be helpful in avoiding war — or further wars once peace has been agreed. South Africa seeks to manage this tension through its Truth and Reconciliation Commission, which offers amnesty in exchange for information to some of those who confess to the crimes of the *apartheid* era. Is this enough? Ntsiki Biko seeks more from her husband's killers: 'How can you forgive without proper justice having been done?' A survey of 20 such commissions around the world paints a very varied picture.[13] In some countries, for example, Uganda and Chile, the impact has been considerable; elsewhere (in Chad, Haiti, and the Philippines) commissions have had very little effect. The variable success of different approaches in Central America points to the need for an effective national process to reveal the culpability for the crimes of the war.

One lesson from many examples is that only when a government is prepared to openly name names, and to give the commission enough resources, can such a mechanism be of significant help. Some have said that what is important is that the truth about the enormities of human rights violations is told, with public admission of who did what; others that knowing is not enough: punishment is needed. Whether or not punishment is always vital, public recognition of and grief over the losses of war, and symbolic reparations by the perpetrators, can help people who have suffered.

But recognising that deep-seated ethnic hatreds increase the risk of war, and that the way both governments and opponents may inflame them can trigger major violence, is only the beginning of a quest for causes. In many wars, the fault-line between combatants is not ethnic at all. In Afghanistan, disputes over land and other issues are fought between members of the same extended family, or *gawm*, who share the same language, religion and ethnicity; and each side enlists ethnic 'others' as their allies;[14] and Africa's wars have been caused by a more complex pattern of events than simple ethnic tension. As Tanzania's former leader, Julius Nyerere, said in December 1996, 'the easily aroused human fears about those who are unlike ourselves in appearance, culture or beliefs' are part, but only part, of any explanation.[15] What kind of a political system makes such hatreds and their manipulation more likely? What kind of an economy denies people peaceful livelihoods and so makes such extremism attractive?

The role of institutions and the state

The lack of a fair and effective rule of law, one of the foundations of democracy, is one condition for violent extremism to flourish. Where states are too corrupt or undemocratic to allow for peaceful change, or have just collapsed as in Somalia or Liberia, violent change becomes almost inevitable. Where there is not an independent and effective judiciary to punish those guilty of gross human rights abuses, this encourages the abusers. Where institutions are too weak to mediate against or to curb unbridled market forces, violent conflict is more likely.

There is no simple way of ensuring that a government is truly accountable to its people. The enthusiasm for so-called 'good governance' after the end of the Cold War was translated too easily into the assumption that Western-style democracy was right for every situation — or in particular, that Western-style multi-party elections would deliver democracy. It has even been suggested that the well-intentioned pressure on the Rwandan government before 1994 to accept swift elections was seen by some leaders as a threat to their power, which persuaded them to choose genocide instead.[16]

While not wishing to question the value of democracy or multi-party elections, the introduction of competitive politics into societies with strong ethnic divisions may do more to increase than to heal divisions, because parties may form and elections be fought along ethnic lines. Prescribing democracy needs therefore to be done with great care, and long-term international support may be needed for countries making the transition from despotism to democracy. Too often, as in Angola, Burundi, or Cambodia, there has been a rapid decline in international support for countries emerging from war, as soon as elections are over.

A culture of violence

Many factors can contribute to creating a 'culture of violence', which can lead to more violence in the home or on the streets, and make major armed violence more likely. Societies differ in the extent to which they encourage young men, in particular, to see violence as a proper and normal tool of living. Brian Keenan's captors in Beirut seemed to be influenced by the curious but deadly combination of watching Rambo films from the United States and listening to the preaching of a particular brand of Islam which justified violence against Western hostages in terms of a struggle for what was believed to be right.

Once a war is formally over, major violence may continue. From the townships of Natal in South Africa to the shanty towns of El Salvador, violence, including domestic violence,[17] can remain the normal way of dealing with tension. There may be cultural reasons for this, including the lack of positive role models for young men; and violence is encouraged by the widespread availability of small arms.

The writer Michael Ignatieff tellingly describes how violence feeds off 'the wild sexuality of the adolescent male'. He summed this up for many current wars:

Children are supplying armies with a different kind of soldier — one for whom a weapon is not a thing to be respected or treated with ritual correctness but instead has an explicit phallic dimension. To traverse a checkpoint in Bosnia where adolescent boys in dark glasses and tight-fitting combat khakis wield AK47s is to enter a zone of toxic testosterone. War has always had its sexual dimension — a soldier's uniform is no guarantee of good conduct — but when a war is conducted by adolescent irregulars, sexual savagery becomes one of its regular weapons.[18]

The media and schools can cometimes play a role in reducing such tendencies. In Mozambique, a television programmge has featured a symbolic burning of children's toy guns (a more dramatic extension of the principle applied by Britain's Early Learning Centre in banning war toys from their shelves). In many countries, there are now spontaneous calls for a morality which is less tolerant of violence — for example, from the Dunblane 'Snowdrop' campaign in Britain, and the People against Human Abuse in South Africa.

Competition for scarce resources

It is perhaps obvious that the scarcer natural resources — land, water, minerals or forests — are, the more intense will be the competition over them, and therefore the more likely it is that such competition will become violent. As suggested above, intense competition without a rule of law, before which all people are equal, too easily becomes violent.

Rwanda and Colombia are just two examples of countries where competition over land, often distributed with gross injustice, can lead to violence, sometimes locally between two families, sometimes nationally or beyond. Competition over water, and control of the flow of rivers, is now seen as a major source of tension, in addition to many others, in the Middle East, where neighbouring countries seldom have a common interest on how, for instance, to dam the Jordan, which Israel has diverted, or the Nile, Tigris or Euphrates. In May 1997, the UN General Assembly agreed guidelines to help countries to resolve their competition over water resources peacefully.

Local conflicts over resources are widespread and have always been so, but there is some evidence that they have become significantly more deadly as guns have replaced traditional weapons, and as established systems of mediating between groups, involving elders and others, have declined. In some cases, such local conflict seems to have been contained locally, and indeed reduced; yet elsewhere local conflict has been linked to a wider war and escalated as a result.

In Sudan in the early 1980s, the Khartoum government conducted its civil war against the Sudan People's Liberation Army by, inter alia, setting up militias of Baggara Arab pastoralists to protect the Bentiu oilfield, and supporting a Nuer force against the SPLA, seen to be dominated by Dinka, traditional rivals of the Nuer. The wider civil war was thus fed by a range of disputes between the different communities, and undermined the traditional ways of resolving ethnic disputes between them. In the 1990s, the splits within the SPLA were along Nuer-Dinka ethnic lines.In Kenya and Uganda, the Turkana and Karomojong compete for scarce water and pastures. In recent years, increasing numbers of both people and livestock have been killed as modern weapons have come in to the area from neighbouring countries. Most of the violence starts as an individual incident which builds up, with revenge and counter-attacks, leading to a wider tribal conflict. By late 1995, scores of deaths were being reported in raids on either side. A series of initiatives then took place to breathe new life into the traditional system of mediation by elders. As a result, there has been a substantial reduction in the number of people and livestock killed.

Population pressure and poverty

The links between population, natural resources, poverty, and violence are complex — and not readily predictable. In many countries, there *can* be a downward spiral of rapid population growth, environmental degradation, and increased poverty, where poor people are concentrated on ecologically fragile and unproductive land. If efforts are not made to break this vicious cycle by tackling poverty and the unequal distribution of resources, improving the status of women, and meeting their reproductive health needs, then pressures may build up and result in armed conflict in some situations.

Rapid populations growth is both a cause and a consequence of poverty. In many sub-Saharan African countries, where poor rural women lose one in three of their children by the end of their child-bearing years, it is hardly surprising that birth rates are high.[19] The demographic history of many developing countries shows that improving education, particularly for women, and providing reproductive health care, and better care for children, can reduce both poverty and birth-rates in a relatively short time. According to the World Bank, fertility rates fall by an average 10 per cent for every year of schooling a woman receives. Educated women are more likely to marry later and have smaller families.[20] The strategy endorsed by the International Conference on Population and Development in Cairo, in 1994, was that better education, health care, and employment opportunities for women will effectively reduce birth-rates.

Inequality and exclusion

If people believe that they are getting a fair share of their society's wealth, they are more likely to feel that they have a stake in it. Former Zaire provides an example of the opposite situation: in early 1997 only one in four people had a job, industry was operating at only 10 per cent of its capacity,[21] and enormous wealth was in the hands of the few. The then President Mobutu's estimated US$ 8 billion fortune, gave a new term to political science: kleptocracy. If a government chooses to siphon off its funds into the foreign bank accounts of its members, to run down public services, and fails to pay its army, it is unlikely to retain much loyalty. Hunger is not so much caused by natural disaster but by state policies. Governments can choose either the 'unaimed opulence' of the few — perhaps why a fifth of Brazilians are hungry — or 'growth mediated security': economic growth for the benefit of all.[22] Effective democracies with a free press tend not to allow governments to ignore their people's need for food.[23] India, for example, was far more successful than, for instance, China in overcoming famine between 1950 and 1980.

A corollary is that large amounts of aid are not by themselves likely to reduce the risk of war. For example, comparatively high levels of development aid went to Somalia and Rwanda only to be wasted. It is the purpose to which aid is put which is significant. If it is not targeted to reduce inequality, nor used as a lever to influence government policies, and if it is given to authorities with poor human rights records, it can indeed do more harm than good.[24] But aid is a relatively small part of the equation compared to trade and investment. Instability, corruption, and lack of infrastructure are blocks to inward investment which can create a self-perpetuating cycle of poverty, conflict, and economic stagnation.

Lack of opportunity

Inequality — relative poverty — does not *cause* war, but it does increase the risk.[25] If men and women have the economic security to feel included in their society, violent conflict is less likely. Where a substantial number do not have the opportunity to earn their own living, it may be a rational decision to join a rebel army or militia, or take part in organised crime. When local youths in the Cibitike area of Burundi's capital, Bujumbura, were no longer employed to clean up the district, the crime rate increased.

This does not only occur in collapsing economies. The situation can be similar in growing economies whose benefits do not reach those on the social margins. The Chiapas revolt in liberalised Mexico shows what may happen where the losers from economic change feel that they have nothing further to lose by fighting the winners. Though the country as a whole is likely to see a net gain from the North American Free Trade Agreement in terms of inward investment, losers include the producers of maize, which is grown on about half of Mexico's agricultural land, and is pivotal to maintaining rural livelihoods. With yields averaging only a fifth of those in the US Mid-West, up to 800,000 small farmers may lose their livelihoods as trade restrictions are removed.[26] Almost a third of the rural population live below the income poverty line, and this situation is likely to worsen in the states of Chiapas, Guerrero, and Yucutan.

Winners and losers in the 'war economy'

Long-running wars may change their nature over the years. The long and bloody path of the Khmer Rouge in Cambodia began as an ideological crusade. Now both the Khmer Rouge and government officials, in collusion, are involved in the illegal felling of timber, which provides both the motive and resources for much of the continued violence. In several other countries around the world, war has become a struggle for control of a lucrative trade in drugs, minerals, or timber, and many other illicit economic activities.

Mao said that it was power which came from the barrel of a gun. So, too, can profit. It is a comforting liberal assumption that nobody benefits from wars. But of course some people do. The leaders who choose the option of war do so because they believe that its benefits (to them) will outweigh its costs. The benefits may not only be political, the acquisition or maintenance of power. Increasingly obvious since the mid-1990s have been the profitable 'war economies' run by businessmen-cum-warlords which help to maintain conflicts from Cambodia to Liberia. Liberia's warring factions make annual profits of tens of millions of dollars from timber, from a significant proportion of the country's trade in diamonds, worth around US$371 million in 1995,[27] and from the extraction and export of gold and rubber.[28]

There are many other examples: Angola's UNITA depends on diamonds; as Filisberto Mateus, a stone-mason employed by Oxfam, put it: 'If the country was poor, they wouldn't be fighting [over it].'[29] The irony is that Angola may be resource rich, but *is* poor — tenth from bottom of the UN's human development index[30] — while many of the fighters on both sides have grown rich from exploiting its natural wealth. Sudanese army officers have made fortunes from dealing in scarce commodities in garrison towns, smuggling and cattle-raiding.[31]

Since the end of the Cold War, many governments and rebels are no longer funded by super-power donors. In Africa in particular, the dire state of government budgets has also pushed soldiers, unpaid for months, into banditry to make a living:

Governments find it more difficult to sustain and control armies, which then turn to local sources of provisioning. These include requisitioning, looting and taxing local populations, involvement in commerce, and diverting humanitarian aid.[32]

This represents in effect the 'privatisation' of African armies, who make money out of their own private business, and often fragment down to local forces controlled by local commanders. Modern war is often the continuation of business, as much as of politics, by other means.[33]

Charles Taylor, leader of the National Patriotic Front in Angola, controls businesses earning an estimated US$75 million a year.[34] For warlords like Taylor, in their search for national political power, economic gain may be only one part of what drives them. But for local factions and individual commanders, the purpose of the war may simply be to make as much money as possible while the war lasts. 'In other words, "war" may dovetail into "crime".'[35]

'Economic gains during civil war can be made from control of the state, from pillage, from charging "protection money" and from control of land, labour, aid and trade.'[36] Some military leaders maintain their power partly because they also provide services to their supporters. They fill the gap left by the decline in government social services. Structural adjustment policies prescribed by international financial institutions have contributed to the decline in public services in many countries. The faction leaders control a web of political, military, and commercial operations, and have responsibilities to give their clients what the state can no longer provide. In Liberia, there has been a variety of mainly informal arrangements between faction members, civil servants, and Liberian-registered companies, often individual expatriate businessmen, with international connections. The link between warlords and civil servants has been strengthened further since the Cotonou Accords divided up all important economic positions in government ministries among the different factions.

International involvement

There have been allegations that Liberia's factions are linked to a series of foreign companies, from Europe, North America, Japan and Malaysia, involved in the extraction and trade in rubber, gold, diamonds, timber, and, till 1993,[37] iron ore.

A similar trend can be seen in some Latin American countries. In Ecuador, Chile, and Honduras, for example, as the military has left government, it has gone increasingly into business. Colombia's army, paramilitaries, and guerillas are all involved in different businesses, not all legal. To some extent, foreign businesses deciding to operate in Colombia have to acknowledge the implications of working in the context of war. Government war bonds are obligatory, and, in practice, paying guerrillas is hard to resist. Both sides demand what amounts to protection money. Beyond that, paying for physical security is part of doing business. British Petroleum and other oil companies directly fund the Colombian armed forces (whose record was condemned in 1996 by the UN Human Rights Commission) to deploy their best troops to protect oil companies' staff, installations, and pipelines. In 1996, the company signed a US$5 million contract with the Colombian army. Amnesty International has emphasised that the company runs the risk of unwittingly contributing to human rights abuses by using the army to protect its installations, particularly as the company has no control over the army's actions. The case has stimulated a new dialogue between the company, Colombian organisations, and several aid agencies, including Oxfam, with all agreeing that there is a need to develop guiding principles to help to guide BP and other companies working in Colombia.

The involvement of international companies in countries at war may provide an opportunity to reduce the effective support for 'war economies' which keep several current wars going. Clare Short, now Secretary of State for International Development, proposed in March 1997 an ethical charter to help the British government to work with business 'to secure development which benefits the poor'. This is part of the larger drive for companies to adopt so-called 'social accounting' or 'social auditing' to measure how well or badly they are doing in helping the people in countries where they operate. A code of conduct for trans-national companies, which Clare Short also proposed, should cover issues of co-operation with combatants in wars, including governments; helping (or at least not hindering) progress on human rights; and in general, how their activities affect countries which may be at risk from war.

Triggers?

So far in this chapter we have looked in broad terms at the factors and trends which increase the risks of war starting and being maintained. Far less obvious are what makes one unstable society erupt into war or genocide, while another, with apparently similar risks, does not. These final 'triggers' of war are more difficult to see,[38] though they crucially include the actions of leaders who calculate that war is in their interest, and who exploit feelings of ethnic or economic exclusion.

Sometimes there may be early-warning signs. When increasing human rights abuses in Rwanda became widely known in 1993, Western governments could have withheld aid. When the UN discovered in Rwanda in early 1994 that there were plans for what the conspirators called 'extermination', and evidence of training and the acquisition of arms to suggest that the plans were well-advanced, these warnings should have been heeded and acted upon.[39]

But the risk factors of ethnic tension, a corrupt state and increasing competition over resources do not explain exactly what prompted the *genocidaires* to carry out their plan. Perhaps the trigger in this case was the proposed system of power-sharing, which could only be prevented through violence. Sometimes it may be that risks which increase rapidly can trigger violence; for example, Albania's pyramid investment schemes collapsed very fast at the end of 1996 and beginning of 1997.

Valpy Fitzgerald, of the UN University World Institute for Development Economics Research, has suggested[40] that it is the inter-actions between three kinds of more or less rapid economic and political change which can turn a conflict-prone country into a war zone. These are, he suggests, first, the sudden widening of inequalities between social, ethnic or territorial groups, increasing the 'losers' sense of injustice. Second, increasingly uncertain economic prospects, heighten-ing people's feelings of insecurity and leading towards aggressive accumulation of wealth. Third, the weakening capacity of the state to maintain law and order, and to mediate between those who have benefited from and those who have been disadvantaged by these changes, by redistributing wealth and being seen to represent the whole of society.

Global factors

Looking further afield, are there global trends which increase some of these risks? Has the ability of people in even the poorest countries to see how the other half of the world, and the other half of their societies, live, through the growth of international media, helped to create aspirations which can only be fulfilled by violent action? Has the fact that economic globalisation has made some richer but others poorer made the latter more likely to resort to war?

The almost universal trend to liberalised economies — encouraged globally through the World Trade Organisation, regionally by the European Union, and by NAFTA and similar agreements in many regions — may increase total wealth, but also threatens the livelihoods of many workers and small producers. Unless that wealth is distributed more equitably, the effect can be to increase, not reduce tensions. It is time for more progress to be made in translating stated commitments on the part of international financial institutions and donors to making poverty reduction central, into concrete action.

The evaluation of the international response to Rwanda's genocide suggested that the impact of adjustment policies and deteriorating terms of trade on unstable countries may be highly damaging, and one factor among others which push a country from instability to war. The end of the International Coffee Agreement in 1989 halved export prices for Rwandan coffee, affecting 70 per cent of rural households, and meant that the government could no longer afford to subsidise farmers as they had in the past. Then in 1990 and 1992, the IMF and World Bank agreed stabilisation and structural adjustment programmes with the Rwandan government, requiring a 50 per cent devaluation and an end to agricultural subsidies. Whether these events increased the risk of war is perhaps not conclusively proven, but they certainly did little to increase the stability of a society which was in a sharp slump from the late 1980s, with GDP collapsing by 40 per cent in the four years to 1993.

Many of the countries at war in the 1990s have been the losers in the global economic changes of the decade. Deflationary economic reform measures without adequate attention to their social effects, and the refusal to speed up reduction of debts, which cost the world's poorest countries in Africa over US$12 billion a year in repayments,[41] do not help to provide the jobs, services, and economic stability needed to build secure and peaceful societies.

Restructuring economies

The same factors which make societies unstable before wars break out also threaten the chances of peace becoming established after the fighting has stopped. This makes a more enlightened approach to post-conflict reconstruction policies of critical importance. In October 1994, Mozambique's multi-party elections were widely praised and seemed to herald a new era of peace, after nearly 20 years of war. But it remains the poorest country in the world, in terms of per capita GNP,[42] and the International Monetary Fund has been criticised for putting fiscal probity before wider security. To get inflation down below 15 per cent, the IMF is said to be discouraging donors from giving enough aid to help in reconstructing the country's economy and services.[43] The government's spending cuts mean that most of the rural health posts, schools, shops, and roads destroyed in the war remain closed. There is no affordable credit for small shopkeepers to reopen the shops buying maize and other crops, and selling salt, cloth and other goods, which have always been at the heart of Mozambique's rural economy.

In the opinion of the Catholic Bishop of Nampula, Manuel Vieira Pinto, 'the IMF must stop looking only at its computers and look at real people... Will all this end violently?' One official of the independent drivers' union, Pedro Chibala, believes the answer is yes: 'Be assured, war will break out again if things don't change.'

Economic policies more sensitive to the risks of war would put a higher premium on reducing inequalities and enabling everyone to have the opportunity of a peaceful livelihood. Unfortunately, the private investment, which is now far more important for the developing world than aid, largely bypasses those countries where, if sensitively used, it could help build such opportunities. In 1996, private investment to developing countries had reached around US$250 million, nearly five times the official global aid total of US$60 million. But the countries which benefit are only those likely to produce a medium-term return. The whole of Africa between the Sahara and South Africa receives less than 2 per cent of the world's foreign direct investment.

For countries more dependent on aid, the situation is bleak. Many of the existing resources are not used well. Oxfam senior policy adviser, Kevin Watkins, criticised the last British government's record in April 1997:

Much of what passes for aid, including the 54 per cent of the budget earmarked for financing the export of British goods, is indefensible. So too is aid to countries such as Indonesia, the fourth largest aid recipient, where the primary purpose is to secure military contracts.[44]

Even within existing resources, there is potential for major improvement; only 10 per cent of Britain's aid budget has been targeted on social priorities. The commitment of the new Secretary of State for International Development, Clare Short, to 'no more Pergaus' represents not just a desire to end the hidden links between aid and arms deals. It also points the way to higher quality aid which is, at the same time, focused on reducing poverty and the risks of war.

The need to focus aid in this way applies both before and after conflicts. The United Nations in Cambodia was criticised for giving too low a priority to social needs. One international official said:

Had the UN spent $2 billion for roads, schools, and rural development rather than on an election, the Khmer Rouge would be weaker in rural Cambodia than they are now.[45]

Cambodia is one of the world's poorest countries today because of the war-damage it has suffered. And as a war-damaged country it needs help to establish a viable, stable economy, and long-term support from donors. Although infrastructure is being rehabilitated with international aid, far more efforts need to be put into rebuilding the production and banking systems. The Cambodian state is not meeting its commitments: spending on education and health remains low, therefore the burden of meeting education and health needs is being borne by international NGOs and humanitarian agencies. The government's resources have gone instead into military expenditure: in 1996, 57 per cent of the national budget (more than half of which is derived from external sources) was spent on defence and security. Illegal logging was another source of revenue for defence.

Effective post-conflict reconstruction in Cambodia should focus on developing the country's human resources, by raising the levels of competence of civil servants — teachers, health workers, agricultural extension workers — to address the lack of motivation and corruption that plagues all government departments. It is also essential to tackle rural poverty, and to strengthen existing democratic institutions.

Practical development projects can have political side-effects. Wells and treatment for schistosomiasis, provided by agencies, can not only help to improve the health of villagers but also, in the words of the regions's deputy governor, 'dry up the Khmer Rouge'.[46]

Though improving the quality of aid is of crucial importance, the decline in quantity of most governments' aid needs to be reversed. Aid for long-term development is at its lowest level for 20 years, and, of this, less and less is spent on countries outside the dynamic regions of the global economy. Government-to-government aid to sub-Saharan Africa fell in real terms each year from 1991–96, taking US$670 million off the amount of aid received.

Disregard for international law

Chapter 2 described how many governments, and those who take up arms against them in the hope of replacing them, routinely and brutally violate the most basic principles of international law. The protection of civilians in war is almost universally ignored.

Some governments neither respect international law, nor see any incentive which would encourage them to abide by its principles. Because the 'international community' does not act consistently to uphold that law, there is an international culture of impunity. Haiti's military who overthrew President Aristide in 1991 taunted the world that they could do what they liked because the UN was too weak to deal with human rights abuses, there or elsewhere. Many of the governments who are the worst offenders against their civilians in wars receive virtually no private investment and minimal international aid; they have no stake in playing by the rules.

Again, there is a positive counter-example. The only region of the world which has gone through the tumultuous changes of post-communist transition without major violence has been the northern half of Central and Eastern Europe, the countries already welcomed into the global economy, and negotiating their entry into NATO and the European Union.[47]

Poland, Hungary, the Czech Republic, and the other Central European countries which have more successfully developed, stake their economic future on their foreign trade and significant inward investment. Having already achieved association agreements, and hoping to join by the turn of the century, EU membership is central to their economic plans. At the same time, membership of NATO, which those three countries are scheduled to achieve by 1999, is vital for their perceived security.

They have made a series of agreements with each other and with the EU on the treatment of their ethnic minorities, precisely because this has been seen as the most likely thing to cause war between them. Perhaps most significantly, the Stability Pact negotiated between the governments of the region and the EU, first proposed by the former French premier Edouard Balladur, explicitly made the chances of gaining admission to the club of wealthier European states dependent on these countries' policies to reduce the risk of war. In short, governments with a stake in being part of the EU or other international clubs may be more likely to adapt their behaviour to fit international standards.[48]

Giving governments in other regions a similar stake, and similar pressure could be a valuable support for the work of people on the ground pressing for change themselves. In May 1997, the UN Security Council discussed the idea that a set of incentives, as well as punishments, should be developed to encourage warring parties to better respect international humanitarian law.

International responsibility

Could a concerted change in economic policy prescriptions really do something to reduce the inequalities and injustices which increase the risk of war? In the mid-1990s, it was difficult to suggest so without seeming idealistic, almost anachronistic. In a move away from the widespread pessimism that nothing can be done, there are now signs of more determined efforts to achieve poverty reduction targets and bring about specific policy changes which could do something to prevent at least some wars.

The Western governments who largely control the international financial institutions seem to lack coherence in their approach. While they call for poverty reduction and the prevention of conflict, they continue to support draconian deflationary economic policies that can have a destabilising effect; they continue to subsidise arms exports, and have not redirected aid. When conflicts occur, they spend sizeable sums on emergency aid and peace-keeping, which may far outweigh the cost of preventive action. This chapter has suggested that the factors which increase the risk of war are many, and complex. However, they are also problems which the international community is committed to addressing: poverty, human rights abuse, discrimination, corruption, and bad governance, which blocks peaceful change. One way to begin, if governments, companies and NGOs are serious about their desire to reduce human suffering in war, would be for each to assess the possible impactof its actions in making conflict more or less likely.

However valuable international action may be, many of the solutions to the problem of war are to be found in the actions of people in the countries affected. Chapter 7 suggests four precise steps which governments could take, but before that, the next chapter looks at the characteristics of stable societies, and at the way in which people in countries experiencing war are taking action to try to resolve conflict, and doing what they can to reduce the human cost of war.

6 Building peace

The risks described in the previous chapter do not inevitably lead to war; the threat of violent conflict can be averted. The strategies to do that must come first and foremost from people in the country concerned, though international action and support may be vital. This chapter will look at what tends to make societies stable, to undergo peaceful change, and avoid violent conflict or repression. It ends with examples of how people in countries affected by war are taking initiatives themselves — which underlines the challenge to the 'international community' to support them in the ways outlined in the final chapter.

Taking responsibility for solutions to conflict

In many regions that have been convulsed by war there is a new determination to find solutions. Africans 'can not simply blame colonialism', one of Oxfam's Tanzanian staff, Ikaweba Bunting, wrote in early 1997. Colonial borders across ethnic lines *are* part of the cause of Africa's recent wars, but

some of the hatred goes back long before then. In Rwanda ... a lot of the problems arose in the context of colonialism [but] nobody made the hand holding the machete rise and fall to kill anybody. These are Africa's problems which have to be sorted out ... [Rwanda's genocide was] like a wake-up call. A bucket of cold water was thrown in people's faces to make them realise what the problems were.[1]

At a different level, Nelson Mandela's international stature has helped to galvanise developments across Africa, including a more effective Organisation of African Unity. In a landmark speech to all African heads of state in 1994, he laid down a challenge to Africans:

We were held up as the outstanding example of the beneficiaries of charity, because we became the permanent victims of famine, destructive conflicts and the pestilences of the natural world. On our knees because history, society and nature had defeated us, we could be nothing but beggars...

Africa cries out for a new birth ... We must face the matter squarely that where there is something wrong in how we govern ourselves, it must be said that the fault is not in our stars, but in ourselves that we are ill-governed. Rwanda stands as a stern and severe rebuke to all of us for having failed to address these matters... [If Africa will] ever know stability and peace ... we must ... bring about an African renaissance.[2]

'Working for a fairer world'

That slogan is how Oxfam recently epitomised its aim: working with people around the world who are striving to tackle poverty and make their societies more prosperous, more equitable, and less at risk of war. Oxfam's experience does not suggest there is any single recipe for success. But it does provide convincing evidence that countries are more likely to be peaceful where strong institutions and the rule of law reduce the incentive to resort to violence — and where an enabling environment provides opportunities for people to gain a livelihood in peaceful ways.

Preconditions for more stable and peaceful societies appear to include:

- An economy whose benefits are distributed equitably enough to provide people with secure livelihoods and a stake in peace.
- A formal government which is representative, not corrupt, responsive to peaceful movements for change, and encourages a sense of national identity while respecting the rights of minorities.
- Vibrant civil organisations representing all sections of society, including both those who may feel excluded and those, including women's groups, who can build bridges between communities.
- An independent and effective judiciary which can punish those guilty of human rights abuses; an impartial police force; and an independent media which can impartially report on abuses.

These are relevant both in countries at risk of war, and also in countries coming out of war seeking a more peaceful future. Just as there is no universal formula for preventing wars, there is no single way to build a peaceful society after a war has ended. But what both successful and failed 'peace processes' do show is that peace can not be built simply on multi-party elections, after which most of the international community make a quick exit. Peace will not endure if the fundamental problems which caused the violence in the first place are not resolved, whether they are racist oppression in South Africa or gross inequalities in access to land and other resources, as in much of Central America.

The next four short sections will look at each of these principles in turn.

An equitable economy

If people have a job, access to decent services, and some say in their future, they may well feel that they have a stake in their society. Governments which work for the many rather than the few (which tend to be democracies) are more likely to provide the services which people demand, and so citizens will feel it is in their interests to maintain the social fabric. In short, a country with effective collective provision for health, education and so on is a country less likely to descend into civil war.

If people have no opportunity for a peaceful livelihood, the choice of anti-social activities becomes an obvious risk. Crime is on the increase in many countries, with the main victims being some of the poorest and most vulnerable people. Sometimes, common crime can become part of the blurred mixture of crime, war, and business characterising 'war economies', as outlined in Chapter 5.

The lack of economic opportunity for many demobilised fighters and others after a peace agreement is signed can present a major threat to a fragile peace. Overcoming these obstacles to peace and stability, both before and after war, requires a commitment to tackle the underlying causes of war and injustice. This in itself can encourage people to believe they have an interest in stability. But it will not happen simply through the workings of the market. As the World Bank *1997 World Development Report* recognised, the state must be capable of setting a legal framework and an economic strategy for successful development. Where state capability has declined, as in many parts of Africa, poverty and the risks of war inevitably increase.

What are required are government policies designed to develop people's skills and capacities, which put a premium on education and health, on spreading the ownership of assets (by land reform, providing access to microfinance, and breaking monopolies), and developing small-scale agriculture and labour-intensive industry. But more particularly, once a war is over, it becomes vital to provide support — training and assistance to develop new livelihood opportunities — to the group who are most likely to make the choice between peace and violence: demobilised fighters.

The politics of inclusion

In countries coming out of war, the victims of violence deserve more than simply economic support. Resources for legal aid and education are vital, as is *some* structure to bring those guilty of war crimes to account. Without this, the complete impunity of mass murderers will help to keep alive deep hatreds, and increase the risk of renewed war.

Tackling the 'culture of violence' which may be endemic, which a war may have built up, and which may have been one of the causes of the war, can also be done through school curricula and the media. Of prime importance are accountable institutions and a political system, which give people a channel for peaceful change, and encourage a sense of civic identity able to embrace the many other identities, social, ethnic and religious, within a state.

Stable democracies do not only depend on electoral systems, but on an active civic life, on people working peacefully together to achieve their goals, and feeling that by doing so they can contribute to political change. People must be free to state their opinions, and confident that what they say will at least be heard without fear or favour.

Citizens for peace

'Civil society' is a concept that has become much discussed in the 1990s. It refers to the amorphous collection of community organisations, NGOs, the media, academics, and private businesses — all the non-state actors that make up a free society, though that distinction can at times be blurred. At its worst, support for civil society has sometimes degenerated into a rather naive assumption that it is inherently 'a good thing', and rather meaningless support for anything which is not run by the government, irrespective of its quality, honesty or who it really represents: 'civil society' can include extremists and groups promoting violence as well as those trying to stop it. What is undeniable is the vital role that some groups and organisations within civil society play in both achieving practical results, and in giving people a peaceful way to express their views and identities. NGOs can help to amplify the voice of minority groups, can bring people from different groups together, and can show an effective way to peacefully influence politics. Thus, 'civil society' can be at the heart of mediating the conflict inherent in changing societies, and in helping to prevent it from becoming violent. In countries emerging from war, civic organisations can help to rebuild the 'social capital' of trust so undermined by war.

Indicting the guilty

Though there may not be a single model for how those guilty of human rights abuses acknowledge their crimes, it is essential that this should happen in some way. The balance between the short-term desire to reconcile bitter enemies, and the need to deal with crimes so that they do not encourage more, may differt from one country to another. The goal should be to build a sustainable peace, not to find a 'quick-fix' in which expediency might suggest that the guilty should escape.

The importance of a system of justice is, of course, far wider than providing an effective way of dealing with war criminals. A stable society requires effective civil policing and a fair and independent judiciary, so that people feel that they do not have to resort to violence to protect themselves or obtain justice. Where a neutral police force has been created after a war, as the PNC was intended to be in El Salvador, this has been crucial to keeping the peace. Nicaragua, by contrast, still suffers widespread violence in rural areas, despite six years of trying to disarm both sides, because people feel they still need their guns in the absence of a civil police.

Independent media, which can speak out against extremists, and exclude malicious propaganda, can be significant in maintaining peace, though like all efforts to end wars, it too can be swamped by dominant hatreds. Both local and international media can be important. Rwanda's virulently anti-Tutsi radios have been countered, at least since 1994, by others promoting ethnic understanding.[3] The Afghan service of the BBC World Service broadcasts a soap opera, based upon *The Archers*, which covers issues arising from Afghanistan's violent conflict in its story-lines.[4]

Support from the international community

Making achievements in each of these areas is fundamentally the responsibility of the people and governments of the countries concerned. Sustainable solutions to war can never be imposed from outside. But the international communit' can, by its actions, either shape an enabling environment in which local efforts for peace are more likely to flourish, or make the risks of violence worse by encouraging the proliferation of arms and the kind of economic development which excludes many people. It is sometimes argued that the term 'international community' has become meaningless. But it is convenient shorthand for the range of external actors (which will vary from one conflict to another) that have the leverage required to bring about change.

International support can come in many forms. From Haiti to central Africa, several recent cases have seen effective activity by private conflict-resolution organisations, such as the Carter Center, led by the former US President, the International Crisis Group, and International Alert, working with local leaders, and groups like Quaker Peace and Service working with lower-level groups. Both to reduce the risks of war, and to relieve its suffering, the work of development and humanitarian agencies can also be crucial — and as Western governments reduce their support, it is such organisations that have sometimes become almost the only mani-festation of the 'international community' in neglected war zones.

Yet it is Western governments, and international institutions — the EU, the World Bank, the UN — which have the greatest influence on shaping an environment which can foster local initiatives to secure peace. As Chapter 4 suggested, positive international involvement has been less than it could have been in the 1990s — while the negative involvement of unregulated arms dealing has been as great as ever.

Complicity or apathy?

Perhaps one of the reasons that there has not been more commitment from Western governments has been that both politicians and the general public have come to see the people caught up in wars around the world as either complicit or apathetic.

People doing little to help themselves has been a stereotype of the victims of the wars and famines of Ethiopia in the mid-1980s or Somalia in the early 1990s. More recently, we have seen the mix of the innocent and guilty among the Rwandan refugees in eastern Zaire. This, for many, has blurred the distinction between the perpetrators of human rights abuses, and their compatriots who failed to oppose them effectively. The conclusion reached is that all have forfeited their rights, and the outside world is absolved from responsibility.

Yet, in every war, there are people taking action to reduce violence and suffering. Even in Rwanda, there were numerous cases of Hutus repeatedly risking their own lives by taking food to hidden Tutsis over the three terrible months of genocide in 1994. Estimates of how many *genocidaires* there were among the genuine Rwandan refugees vary enormously from 20,000 to more than ten times that number. Yet even the highest figure amounts to no more than a quarter of the 1.2 million who fled Rwanda for former Zaire in 1994. The killing in Rwanda, and the difficulty of distinguishing between some combatants and non-combatants in guerrilla warfare, referred to in Chapter 2, shows that wars can erode moral judgement. But the writing-off of the majority of civilians as somehow 'guilty' of the violence around them is not thereby justified.

Active peace-making

In every society at war there will be people trying to find a solution to both the war and the problems which have led to it. As one eminent analyst of African affairs observed in 1996: 'Nothing empowers people quite like their own survival.'[5]

In Burundi's capital, Bujumbura, the residents of two *quartiers*, one predominantly Hutu, one Tutsi, work together to seek some form of security. Through an ethnically-mixed committee of 55 men and women, the two communities of Kinama and Cibitoke have agreed to try to protect each other from attack, whether from Burundi's army or rebels. The fighting which has dominated the country almost continuously since October 1993 has cost the lives of four members of the committee, but this initiative is having some effect in reducing the violence in at least one part of the capital.

In Ghana, local and international NGOs banded together in an NGO consortium to work with communities on all sides of the violent conflict to make opportunities for negotiation and peaceful resolution. NGOs, community leaders, and government authorities were brought together to discuss the claims by one marginalised group, which was at the root of the conflict, and to pressure the government to acknowledge and respond to those claims.[6] Bottom-up processes are not sufficient to secure peace, but they do seem to be a necessary condition for higher-level peace-making.

Each year since 1992, in Cambodia, hundreds of Buddhist monks and others have walked 340 kilometres on a 24-day 'peace walk' from the Thai border to Phnom Penh.[7] The walk was initiated to provide 'a ray of hope at a difficult time'. The risks they were taking in demonstrating for peace were tragically clear in 1994 when one of the walkers was killed in crossfire between Khmer Rouge and government soldiers. Happily, the 1997 walk, in March, passed off without attack.

Those working for peace and justice for their communities can put themselves at enormous personal risk. Increasingly in Colombia, the leaders of peasant and human rights groups, and trade unions, have to flee their homes after receiving threats from paramilitaries linked to the Colombian armed forces.[8] In May 1997, three people linked to the Centre for Popular Education and Investigation were murdered in a Bogota flat.

One of the most promising initiatives in Colombia has been the growth of so-called 'communities of peace': groups declaring that they are neutral in the fighting between military, paramilitaries, and guerrillas. Many of these peace communities have been developed by the comparatively small number of Colombia's indigenous Indians. In the Antioquia department, which has 17,000 Indians belonging to five ethnic groups, the level of violence has increased since 1994. The army accuses civilians of supporting the guerrillas, demands that they leave their land, and restricts the delivery of food. A number of Indians have been murdered, including 12 community leaders in the Chigorido area, since 1994.[9] The Antioquia Indigenous Organisation, which Oxfam supports, combines practical help in the form of food, shelter and medicine for people who have been forced off their land, with the use of radio, television and the press to proclaim their neutrality.[10] In another community of peace, San José de Apartadó, 37 members have been killed since declaring neutrality. Particularly without an international presence to observe, local initiatives to reduce violence often demand enormous courage.

Around the world, people may be forced to negotiate with the killers to save their lives. Even in the bloody war in Liberia, this has sometimes been successful when the fighters can see that they gain more by letting people live. In April 1997, Tenneh Sirleaf explained to the National Human Rights Monitors of Liberia, who Oxfam works with, what had happened in the town of Tahn:

When we learned of the advance of the rebels on our town, we organised ourselves into a community watch team with two responsibilities. First, to keep an outpost [to watch] for the rebels' advance and solicit information about their activities. And secondly, to negotiate with the rebels for the security of the town...

We fetched food, water, and other essential goods for them. Through this, we were able to secure our town from mayhem and destruction. Even though there were some instances of violence, this method worked well ... to reduce and prevent further violence.[11]

One of the profound though intangible effects of many wars is that the unifying force of nationalism can reduce popular concern for social reform, human rights or gender equality. This is not inevitable; the second world war in Britain is often cited as an example of a war during which a sense of community was created which actually increased the pressure for social change. In parts of former Yugoslavia in the 1990s, some groups have worked for years to counter the prevailing ethnic hatreds. Every week throughout the wars, a group of 'Women in Black' demonstrated in Belgrade's central square for mutual tolerance.[12] In the majority-Albanian region of Kosovo, the women's group, Motrat Qiriazi, has campaigned against discrimination and violence, despite repeated threats from the Serbian police. Part of Oxfam's work in Serbia, Croatia, and Bosnia is to help to bring these groups together with others across former Yugoslavia, to build up the trust between different ethnic groups which is such a casualty of war.[13]

Strengthening traditional systems of mediation

Traditional communities have often developed effective means of resolving conflict, both within that community and with neighbours. But as social patterns change under pressures of modernisation and economic development, structures such as village councils may no longer function effectively. Reviving these community systems of mediation can sometimes be an effective means of resolving current conflicts.

Community leaders from both sides of Mali's conflict have formed so-called 'peace cells' to resolve inter-communal disputes. This has been *one* critical strategy in bringing Mali back from the brink of worsening conflict. The initiative has built on, not replaced, traditional ways of dealing with tensions, including the web of alliances which cross ethnic groups and families, known as 'cousinage'.

Elders who used to pacify conflicts between Turkana and Karomojong in Central Africa over the use of water and pasture land, seemed to have lost some of their authority to formal government structures, which could not themselves bring peace. During 1996, the two governments, Kenya and Uganda, and international NGOs helped to bring together more than 50 elders who agreed to return abducted children and stolen livestock, and make compensation for human lives which had been lost during recent cross-border disputes between the two communities. There is now a strong 'border peace committee' involving both communities, with some elders entrusted with the task of preserving the peace. Petty theft continues, but there are now far fewer deaths.

Helping themselves and one another

The image of a helpless, dependent refugee, which aid agencies, including Oxfam, have helped to popularise, is another stereotype which can be far from reality. Though humanitarian aid can mean the difference between life and death for many, refugees are frequently earning their own precarious livelihoods within the limited possibilities open to them. In 1993, a study of Ethiopians in Somalia put it this way:

Not only did the refugees seize every available opportunity to earn an income, but they also [contracted with local farmers] to gain access to land and employment. More often than not these were inequitable relationships ... but ... they provided the refugees with a means to engage in productive activities, no matter how infinitesimal were the returns.[14]

In the town of Monteria, near Colombia's Atlantic coast, mothers of families which have fled their homes set up 'community kitchens' to improve their children's nutrition, giving food and advice to the newly displaced, and helping those affected by the floods of 1995.[15] In Cambodia, refugees are returning to cultivate the land as more of the country is freed from Khmer Rouge control. Sourn Sea is 42 and returned to the village of Kandal in 1992 after 13 years as a refugee on the Thai border. Though he lost both his legs from a landmine, he works the land from his wheelchair to support his family:

We have just the plot the house is on. We rent a hectare of land from a villager to grow rice. We borrowed money from CFDS (an Oxfam-supported project) to pay for the ploughing, and got rice seed from another organisation. I can do most agricultural work except ploughing. We had to take our eldest daughter out of school to help earn money, but I hope that we will be able to keep the others there.

Our village leader has told us that now the Khmer Rouge are no longer a threat, there are 120 hectares of land, 4 kilometres away, which he will give to returning families like us. There are about 120 families here so we will get a hectare of land each. That's not enough to live on, but it will be a great improvement in our lives. I don't know when we will get the land — the sooner the better. We will have waited 5 years.[16]

UNHCR acknowledges that most refugees go home on their own feet or by their own efforts, not in transport supplied by the High Commissioner. In 1994, 624,500 Mozambicans returned from Malawi, virtually half a million of them without any help from UNHCR. In the same year, 92,600 Afghans went home from Pakistan, more than two-thirds of them without official assistance. Those that UNCHR itself repatriates are equally independent:

When, after years of living in exile, refugees calmly disembark from the bus, truck or boat which has brought them back to their homeland, [they] pick up their meagre belongings and a modest package of assistance, walk back to their village and start to pick up the pieces of the life they left behind.[17]

Before they get home, many who have fled their homes and sometimes their countries are housed and helped by local people rather than international organisations. Much of the help to Colombia's displaced people is given by small local organisations, usually working with 50 to 100 families, and offering some basic goods, health care and legal advice.[18]

In many poor countries, the extended family provides a vital safety-net. Pithule fled the fighting between the government and Karen separatists in Myanmar (Burma) and found her distant family in Thailand:

The house we live in, and this building which we use as a weaving centre, belong to a sympathetic Thai, a relative — my daughter-in-law's aunt. The big advantage is that we have the space to set up the looms so we can weave cloth and make things for sale.[19]

People also help each other to cope with the psychological suffering which wars inflict. In Kinyarwanda, the language of Rwanda, 'agahozo' roughly translates as 'you wipe away my tears, I wipe away yours'. In other words, mutual support. It is also the name of an organisation, set up in 1994 by women in Kigali who, as they struggled among the bodies to discover their dead, also discovered that they were not alone.[20] Many of them had been raped, and had also lost their children and husbands.

At the beginning, some of their work was simply to help each other bury their dead, and to gain support from sharing their different, but similar, horrific experiences. From a handful, the group soon grew to more than 50 in Kigali, and joined up with similar efforts throughout Rwanda. Oxfam's Esther Mujawayo, who lost her own husband and more than 30 relatives in the genocide, travelled around Rwanda, encouraging widows to come together to help each other. Now more than 9,800 women are involved. The benefits they have gained include obtaining material to build their own houses, training for their new roles as heads of households, in new skills for new employment, and counselling for the trauma of the events of 1994.

Linking rights and responsibilities

In 1995, 28 eminent people from almost as many countries, and all continents, collaborated to publish a report, *Our Global Neighbourhood*, which argued that the only hope for a more peaceful and prosperous world was a range of international reforms based on 'a common commitment to core values that all humanity could uphold'. Everyone, it said, had a common set of rights and responsibilities, a right to 'a secure life' — but also a responsibility not to harm 'the security and welfare of others'.[21]

Though Nelson Mandela said at the time that 'we will turn to [*Our Global Neighbourhood*] again and again', the idea that rights and responsibilities are linked has hardly featured in the political or media debate on how we can respond to wars. Yet in Oxfam's vision of what an ethical foreign policy could mean, this is crucial. The rights so regularly violated in modern wars are basic foundations of what the international community claims to believe in. They are what women, men, and children are universally entitled to. In claiming those rights, civilians are taking on a responsibility not to violate the rights of others. Most fulfil that responsibility. That places a parallel responsibility upon every one of us to do what we can to help civilians enjoy those basic rights which wars violate.

The final chapter sets out the four areas in which the international community, particularly governments, could take action in support of international law, both to reduce the risk of war, and to protect the rights of civilians.

7 A better way?

There is a better way than what has been called 'the bland statements, half-promises and betrayals' of the international response to conflict in the 1990s.[1] But it will only come about through many people taking up their responsibilities to help others enjoy their rights.

There is no single panacea to the problem of war. Julius Nyerere, Tanzania's former President, now involved in mediation in Central Africa, said in December 1996:

Endeavours to assist in the making of peace would not be necessary if there were easy answers to the deep-seated fears, suspicions and prejudices which lead to violence.[2]

But there are a range of effective and practical policy changes which, if coherently applied, could significantly reduce the suffering and destruction caused by armed conflict. Most of these need to be undertaken by the governments and others in countries at war. But many others are the responsibility of those powerful governments which dominate international relations and control the resources needed to invest in peace. Most of the recommendations could be achieved by the better targeting of existing resources. Others require new expenditure, but would prove to be prudent investments if they successfully reduced some of the huge costs — financial as well as human — of failing to prevent wars.

In the following four areas, governments could make a significant impact in protecting civilians in war:

Curb the arms trade:
- Regulate the arms trade with both a European Union and an international code of conduct to prevent arms flows to where they are likely to be used to kill civilians.
- Increase the effort to suppress the illegal arms trade, through implementing the 1997 EU Programme for Combating Illegal Trafficking in Conventional Arms, and similar measures in other regions.

- Press for effective international de-mining — and a verified international ban on all anti-personnel mines.

Bring war criminals to justice:
- Set up an International Criminal Court to prosecute and deter genocide, mass murder, rape as a weapon of war, and all crimes against humanity. In order to be effective, it would need to have the independent right to prosecute all war crimes, and be backed by the political will and resources of governments.

Promote peace:
- Audit all international economic, trade, aid and investment policies which may affect vulnerable countries through a 'conflict impact assessment'.

Uphold the rights of refugees and other civilians:
- Press the UN Security Council to take effective steps to help to prevent wars and protect civilians, including considering the options of a UN Centre for Conflict Prevention to recommend consistent, timely, and proactive measures; and develop more transparent ways of working.
- Ensure that emergency aid meets agreed 'humanitarian standards' for refugees, internally displaced people, and all civilians, and provides a 'net benefit' in maximising efforts to save lives and protect basic rights.
- Review British asylum and social security policies to ensure fair treatment for individuals seeking refuge

A global neighbourhood?

One of the most contentious issues in reducing wars is the appropriate role of outsiders, be they neighbouring governments, regional powers, the UN Security Council, the most powerful governments, or NGOs. Because the 'international community' got it so wrong, overall, in Somalia, Bosnia and Rwanda, by the mid-1990s it had become fashionable to argue that there was little that outside governments could usefully do. The record of outside involvement in the wars of the 1990s, even leaving aside the supply of arms, has been marked by inaction and lack of interest. As Sadako Ogata said at the Holocaust Memorial Museum in April 1997: 'Bosnians and Rwandans perished because the major powers saw no strategic interest in helping them.'[3]

There is no excuse for misplaced and partisan strategies like the disproportionate force against Aideed's supporters in Somalia in 1993.

But there are reasons of both morality and enlightened self-interest why the international community must become more engaged in finding effective solutions to future wars. Morally, governments which by virtue of their regional or international influence, or relative capacity, particularly the permanent members of the Security Council, can do something to prevent wars or protect civilians within them, have a responsibility to do so. But, in an increasingly interdependent world, where their prosperity depends on the ability to trade peacefully, and their long-term credibility on whether the Security Council, for example, will fulfil its mandate, it is also in the longer-term interests of those governments to adopt more proactive foreign policies than the ones seen in the past few years.

Yet if 'something must be done', it is well to be realistic and humble about what that something can be — and more particularly to remember that the role of outside powers is almost always to support, not replace, the initiatives of people in the countries at war, or in neighbouring countries. There have been too many examples of inaccurate assessments of rapidly-changing situations, and predictions leading to damaging policies. The starting point for any attempt to prevent conflict is to be fully aware of the local situation. NGOs as well as global institutions like the World Bank and the IMF have sometimes got it wrong by pushing a 'global solution' — such as, a draconian stabilisation and adjustment plan that does not take sufficiently into account the explosive social impact on the poorest and most marginalised.

Even with far better analysis, the prevention and resolution of wars is exceedingly difficult. Only 15 per cent of the civil wars of the twentieth century have been resolved through peace settlements.[4] All the rest have been fought until one side was vanquished — or, like many, are still going on, as in Sudan, Afghanistan or Colombia.

There is a need for greater international support for local initiatives seeking solutions to wars, including those by organisations within 'civil society', as outlined in the previous chapter; and for peace initiatives by governments and regional bodies, accompanied by a more proactive and principled international policy.

Conflict-impact assessment

Before looking at each of the four steps suggested above in more detail, it must be stressed that *any* change in policy should be continuously assessed for its impact on increasing or reducing the risks of war.

In March 1997, Clare Short, now British Secretary of State for International Development, proposed that her new Department for International Development should work with business and others to ensure that both government and private investment overseas should be 'socially audited'. This is vitally important not just to help in reducing poverty, but also to reduce the risks of war.

For governments, one way to do this would be to include such audits in the annual reports of the foreign, trade, finance, defence, and development ministries to parliaments, or in the remits of parliamentary committees or government offices monitoring different departments' performance. Included in any such assessments should be a measurement of performance against the relevant parts of international law, including the Geneva Conventions, Genocide and Refugee Conventions.

This approach could usefully be applied by all governments, and by regional organisations like the European Union or the Organisation of African Unity, and indeed by the United Nations. Nor should NGOs be immune from more open assessment. Wherever there is not a culture of transparent evaluation, or where politicians, officials, or aid workers, are not held to account for their performance, there is an urgent need for this kind of reform.

Clare Short's proposals, updated in a speech in July 1997, also reflect the growing realisation that in a world where aid is a fraction of private and foreign direct investment, only a private-public partnership can effectively provide international support for development. Private investment has produced major benefits, but has also sometimes been linked to the tangled relationships of 'war economies', or helped to prop up governments with poor human rights records. There is therefore scope for some form of code of conduct, independently verified, which companies investing in countries at risk of war are encouraged to adopt. Perhaps most crucially, the private export of arms is in urgent need of effective regulation. The relevant section below outlines several recent practical proposals on how this might be done, to ensure that the end-users of the arms sold do not use them to kill civilians.

More open assessment of the impact of policies in making war more or less likely would be a new way of working for most governments, businesses, and aid agencies alike, one which will be vitally important in the coming years. But there are four immediate steps which governments could take:

Curb the arms trade

This would include:

- Regulating the arms trade with both a European Union and an international code of conduct to prevent arms reaching areas where they are likely to be used to kill civilians.
- Increasing the effort to suppress the illegal arms trade, through implementing the 1997 EU Programme for Combating Illicit Trafficking in Conventional Arms, and similar measures in other regions.
- Pressing for effective international de-mining — and a verified international ban on all anti-personnel mines

Regulation

There is an urgent need to regulate the international arms market both to prevent the arms and ammunition reaching areas where they are likely to be used against civilians — and to discourage the waste of resources on excessive military spending which could otherwise be invested in social and economic development. In May and June 1997, the US House of Representatives voted for a code of conduct to regulate US exports, the British Foreign Secretary announced that a similar code would be a priority for the UK Presidency of the European Union in 1998, and seven Nobel Peace Laureates, led by Dr Oscar Arias, proposed an international code to build on these initiatives, to be agreed by the UN by the end of the century. South Africa, Africa's biggest arms exporter, is also considering the introduction of regulations similar to those in the US and EU codes.

The detail of policy should follow the UK Government's existing sense of where the onus of proof should lie. There should be no sales to any group which *might* use them to abuse human rights, for internal repression or external aggression. It can be reasonably assumed that arms *might* be used in this way if the users have, for example, a poor record on human rights, whether or not they have used the same type of weapon in this way before.

It will be important to ensure that the codes agreed lead to actual restrictions on the supply, and are not set at a lowest common denominator between, for example, the widely varying policies of the main European producers. Enforcement will only be possible with the commitment of governments, and their willingness to focus on the small arms, including those surplus from declining Western armies, which, in practice, account for most deaths in current conflicts, as well as the more lucrative major weapons systems.

Suppression of the illegal trade in arms

Together, the EU and US account for 80 per cent of the legal market, but perhaps the majority of small arms are transferred around the world illicitly. This includes the so-called 'grey' market in arms exported legally from major arms-exporting countries, but then sold on and on to others with no controls. The EU Programme for Combating Illicit Trafficking in Conventional Arms was agreed in June 1997 at the initiative of the Dutch Presidency, and includes the twin objectives of bringing together more effective police and customs operations in Europe, and supporting other countries to control their borders, and suppress the trade, including programmes to 'buy back' weapons from combatants. This, particularly if it feeds into coherent support for countries emerging from conflicts, is an important step. Producer countries have a responsibility for the end use of their arms; their embassies could at least do 'spot checks' to help to verify this, and investigate more fully suspected abuses. This would be much easier if governments also established some system of registering and tagging new arms and ammunition.

Since some of the applicants for EU membership from Central and Eastern Europe, including the Czech Republic, are reported to be among the centres for the illegal arms trade, the EU should make it an absolute condition for membership that these governments, if necessary with EU support through its PHARE or TACIS programmes (aid to the central and eastern European countries and the former Soviet Union, respectively) demonstrate their determination to effectively curb this trafficking as well as tighten regulations on their legal trade. Without such a firm line, there could be an increasing problem as new NATO members upgrade their weapons and recoup the cost by selling off their old stock.

A ban on landmines

In January 1995, no government in the world was committed to banning anti-personnel mines. It now looks certain that a large number will soon have pledged themselves to do this through the so-called 'Ottawa process'. Led by Canada, they include both producers as well as countries affected by mines; 41 of Africa's 52 countries had agreed to a ban by May 1997, along with all but three of NATO's members. It will then be important that those governments pushing for a ban apply consistent pressure on others, through conditions on aid and trade preferences, to extend the ban to all producers.

Yet since there are already enough mines in the ground to go on killing for 50 years, clearing existing mines, and supporting the victims of mines with training and other help to enable them to make a livelihood, are also vital. There is a real impact from effective mine-clearance: 100,000 Cambodian refugees have been able to go home since 1993.[5] More could be done with increased investment as part of post-conflict reconstruction and development programmes.

Bring war criminals to justice

This would include:

- Setting up a permanent International Criminal Court to prosecute and deter genocide, mass murder, rape as a weapon of war, and all crimes against humanity.
- Ensuring its effectiveness by giving it the independent right to prosecute all war crimes, and the backing of political will and resources of governments.

A permanent international court

Almost 50 years after the idea was first proposed, in the aftermath of the Tokyo and Nuremburg trials, a permanent court to deal with war crimes may finally be established before the end of the century. It is vitally important for the international community to do so, to send a clear message to those who commit appalling acts, in their quest for economic or political gain, that such crimes will be punished.

Yet the problems of both incompetence and lack of funding which have plagued the current tribunals on Rwanda and former Yugoslavia provide a warning that if this project is eventually to be implemented, it must be done well. By March 1997, the International Tribunal on former Yugoslavia had only indicted 74 suspects, and the tribunal on Rwanda a derisory 21. Of these, 75 remain free.[6]

Any such court will only be as effective as the will of governments and competence of the UN human rights machinery makes possible. Neither has been particularly evident in the past. In 1997, UN Secretary-General Kofi Annan has taken several steps to improve matters: a tough crack-down on corruption and incompetence in the UN Rwanda tribunal; and appointing the high-profile Irish President, Mary Robinson, as the next UN High Commissioner for Human Rights, and merging her office with the Centre for Human Rights.

The court should be able to try individuals acting for any organisation: governments, rebel movements or indeed UN peace-keepers who violate those they are supposed to protect. It is planned that the court will deal with war criminals in both civil and international wars. The signal that governments are determined to see this done would be increased if those countries which have still not ratified the relevant 1977 Second Protocol to the Geneva Conventions did so now.

Individual states should not have the power to block the courts' jurisdiction. Though the International Criminal Court should essentially fill the gaps where national courts are unable or unwilling to try international crimes, the court must have the right to independently investigate whether the national jurisdiction has in fact been independently carried out.

To make it accessible to those who are victims of war crimes, the court will require the right to initiate investigations based on information from any source, including individuals and groups within civil society, and not only from governments.

Rape as a weapon of war

To try to reduce sexual violence in war, it will also be important that the permanent court, like its temporary predecessor on Rwanda and former Yugoslavia, states that rape, forced prostitution and other acts of sexual violence are grave breaches of the Geneva Conventions — and takes strong action against the perpetrators.

In 1998, the UN Commission on the Status of Women — set up at the 1995 Beijing Conference on Women — is due to examine ways in which violence against women can be reduced. It is to be hoped that they will suggest practical steps which could be taken to reduce sexual violence as a military tactic.

Promote peace

This would include:

- Auditing all international economic, trade, aid, and investment policies which may affect vulnerable countries through a 'conflict impact assessment'

- Governments, companies, NGOs and all relevant bodies should be able to demonstrate that their policies pass such an assessment

Auditing policies

In the words of British Foreign Secretary, Robin Cook, speaking in 1994:

The message from the conflict born of poverty is that international security is best built on international solidarity, in which the wealthiest nations help the poorest out of the poverty that breeds conflict.

This requires all relevant policies to be tested against their impact on making countries more or less stable. It is beyond the scope of this book to suggest in any detail what such policies would be. (The *Oxfam Poverty Report*, published in 1995, deals with many of them more fully.) However, considering those factors which increase the risks of wars would lead to the redesign of international economic policy to give far higher priority to reducing poverty in unstable countries, and more generous support for reconstruction in countries emerging from war.

Reforming trade policies

Far more than aid, it is trade, on fair terms, and other international economic policies, which can help to deliver the more equitable economic climate which can increase people's stake in peace. The international financial institutions have a role to play, particularly the World Bank, which needs to be encouraged by its shareholders to demonstrate that poverty reduction is central to its mandate, and the IMF, which should change its insistence on deflationary monetarist policies that may ignite social tensions.

The international trade rules administered by the World Trade Organisation need to be fundamentally changed. They currently allow protection for some while pressing extreme deregulation for others. By demanding that all governments protect basic labour rights as a condition of membership, the benefits of the global economy would be more fairly shared. An international trading regime which was sensitive to the risks of war could offer the least developed countries — often those at most risk — various trading preferences including zero tariffs and more flexible rules of origin. The World Trade Organisation's Plan of Action to promote trade capacity-building and favourable market access for the least developed countries is therefore to be welcomed.

Transnational corporations and others which are sensitive to their responsibilities will wish to develop codes of conduct to guide their work in vulnerable countries, which should include commitments to fair trading as well as suggesting ways in which they might exert an influence to improve human rights performances.

Reducing debt

Debt is a millstone around the necks of Sub-Saharan and other least developed countries at risk of war. The debt of the 41 highly indebted poor countries now totals US$215 billion, up from US$183 billion in 1980. Though the recent multilateral initiative to provide debt relief to these countries is welcome, the relief will be selective, and often take from three to six years to have any effect. Swifter and more effective action, rather than further proposals, are what is required. Debt relief is a vital way to reduce poverty in these countries, provided the benefits of debt relief are channelled to fund education, health care, microfinance, and rural development programmes which target the poorest.

Better-targeted aid

High-quality, poverty-focused official aid, though proportionately less important than investment, still has a vital role to play. Investing in aid for social development, if targeted to reduce inequalities, is investing in stability. This means focusing aid where it has a real impact for the many.

To any country which may be vulnerable to new or renewed violence, development strategies should also include what has become known as the 'security first' approach, in which support for buying up and destroying weapons, and economic alternatives for demobilised fighters, are priorities for international support.

Aid should be regarded as a catalyst which can create an enabling environment for the private investment which dwarfs it. Improving the quality of aid so that 20 per cent is spent on basic social needs, while pressing receiving governments to spend at least 20 per cent of their budgets in the same way, is an achievable start.

The growth of so-called 'conditionalities' on aid in the 1990s should be extended to include the condition that receiving governments are not pursuing policies likely to increase the risk of war. If a government is violating human rights, or distributing its public spending in a grossly biased way, to favoured regions, ethnic groups or political supporters, it is promoting tension, and can not expect aid donors to support it.

Governments can not expect aid if they are spending far more on their military than can be justified by a reasonable assessment of threats to security. Aid donors have a similar responsibility in respect of their spending. Conditions for aid should be consistently applied across countries, and support be given to those governments genuinely trying to build the kind of institutions, such as an independent judiciary, which are the foundations of a peaceful society, and which Western donors rightly demand.

In particular, the Group of Eight leading industrialised powers need to show leadership in pressing for the kind of economic policies outlined above, and for a new aid compact combining social and economic progress. This could aim to achieve the Organisation of Economic Cooperation and Development's targets for access to primary education and primary health care by 2015, and a fall of two-thirds in child and infant death rates.

Uphold the rights of refugees and other civilians

This would include:

- Pressing the UN Security Council to take effective steps to help to prevent wars and protect civilians, including considering the options of a UN Centre for Conflict Prevention to recommend consistent, timely, and proactive measures; and to develop more transparent ways of working.
- Ensuring that emergency aid meets agreed 'humanitarian standards', for refugees, internally displaced people and all civilians, and provide a 'net benefit' in maximising efforts to save lives and protect basic rights.
- For Britain, there should be a review of asylum and social security policies to ensure fair treatment for individuals seeking refuge.

Reform of the Security Council

The Security Council has often failed in its admittedly awesome mission to save the world 'from the scourge of war'[7] because of various combinations of the lack of early warning and failure of political will. The latter has been by far the most critical. The gross inconsistency between the way in which crises in Albania, for example, and some African countries, are handled, seems as stark in 1997 as ever. This, along with the traditionally closed way in which the Council's permanent members have done their business, has contributed to a decline in credibility which is bad both for the Council and its member governments.

In 1996, the British Labour Party proposed 'a new high-profile Centre for Conflict Prevention within the UN Secretariat'.[8] Its purpose could be two-fold. It could provide sound analysis, using all available information (including from the UN, governments, and aid agencies), and, through the authority of the Secretary-General, present precise recommendations for consistent action to the Security Council. Some of the Council's members have found it too easy to evade responsibility by claiming ignorance. The Centre's recommendations, presented by an activist Secretary General, could do much to help the Security Council take well-informed and timely decisions.

Several Security Council members have stressed their desire to be better informed of the humanitarian consequences of both action (such as sanctions) and inaction. The February 1997 presentations by Oxfam's David Bryer and two other NGO leaders, and the involvement of other humanitarian agencies in a Council debate in May 1997, may have marked the start of a very welcome new trend. The 1996 evaluation on Rwanda[9] suggested that there could also be a more structured way to ensure the Council had all the information it needed — a humanitarian sub-committee, including sufficiently senior members of the Council, which would report to the full Security Council on all relevant matters.

Sanctions

It would be for such a group, for example, to improve the way in which the Council uses sanctions. The current cost-benefit of sanctions is tragically unbalanced. By late 1995, a UN study estimated that up to half a million children may have died as a result of the economic sanctions imposed after Saddam Hussein's invasion of Kuwait in August 1990.[10] It took almost seven years, till March 1997, before the first supplies — of chick peas and vegetable oil — reached Iraq as part of the 1996 deal to sell some oil for food and medicine.[11]

No sanctions should be imposed without constant monitoring of their impact on civilians. In an Oxfam lecture in Oxford in 1996, Chile's ambassador to the United Nations, Juan Somavia, one of the Security Council's temporary members, set out a practical six-point plan to make sanctions compatible with humanitarian action, which should be urgently considered. The spirit of Somavia's proposals is summed up in his second point: to punish the rulers not the ruled:

Sanctions should be primarily addressed to the leaders in conflict by targeting them on the military and civilian structures that support the regime and on the factions, groups and warlords that are parties to a civil war ... We need to shift the impact of sanctions from the people at large to the leaders, in particular through, among other means, measures related to bank accounts, commercial interests, stocks and properties in foreign countries, residence status and visas.[12]

A better use of sanctions could be part of the more coherent and decisive use of diplomatic and other measures — from aid conditionality to peace-keeping — in the face of major human rights abuses. It should be possible for the Security Council to show firm leadership. But that will require real change, both in its ways of working and in its membership. The Centre for Conflict Prevention, for example, could help to demonstrate that future decisions are transparently taken based on open and impartial analysis, not just from the closed discussions of the permanent five, and sometimes less. After years of discussion, there is now the possibility that the Council's membership will be reformed in the next few months.[13] The question of membership must be resolved if the Security Council in the next century is to be seen as having legitimacy as a representative body of international opinion. But most important of all are consistent efforts to protect civilians.

Standards for humanitarian relief

With several other aid agencies, Oxfam has committed itself to develop and maintain precise standards of entitlements in emergencies. NGOs and official aid donors should commit themselves to humanitarian standards and push for them to be upheld by all channels — such as voluntary organisations, UN agencies, and the EU — through which relief funds pass. The international development departments could include their performance against these standards as part of annual 'audits' to parliament (see above); these standards are of course a practical reflection of the rights to humanitarian relief in international law.

Neither aid agencies nor governments will be able to meet these standards without remedying some of the injustices of the current aid system. People who flee wars within their countries, and those who do not flee at all, should receive the same quality of aid as those who are technically refugees outside their homelands. Aid agencies should be acutely aware of the specific needs and specific voice of women, and women should be protected by being granted refugee status in their own right, not through their husbands or fathers. Donors and UNHCR should continue to supply aid to refugees until they can return to their countries through their own free will, rather than following the recent trend of reducing relief to effectively force people home.

In July 1997, Kofi Annan concluded the latest assessment of UN reform. In proposals for improving the performance of its humanitarian agencies, to be discussed by governments in the General Assembly in October 1997, he opted for what is essentially the present system of independent UN agencies with a central Emergency Relief Co-ordinator. If an improvement is to result, it may largely depend on whether the person appointed is given sufficient power to co-ordinate the disparate agencies effectively, to adjudicate between them when they disagree, and to speak with a powerful voice, to become a forceful humanitarian advocate at the most senior level of the UN. The loophole that leaves 19 million internally displaced people unprotected should be addressed by including them within UNHCR's mandate.

UK asylum law

Both the way in which applications for asylum are dealt with and the benefits available to refugees have been significantly changed in the 1990s. The overall aim of the British government regarding asylum-seekers should be to review the current situation and develop a comprehensive framework to ensure that every asylum-seeker is dealt with fairly, and that once asylum-seekers are granted refugee status, they are given support to settle. This should be done in the context of an overall levelling-up of standards throughout the EU, which would include the right of asylum-seekers to have their application heard in the EU country of their choice,[14] and the recognition of gender persecution against women as a legitimate reason for seeking asylum. The British government could take the lead in pressing for a reform of asylum and immigration policies across the EU, with a view to matching the highest standards of fair treatment, as set out in UNHCR guidelines.

There are three specific concerns regarding the way asylum-seekers are currently treated in the UK:

- About 800 asylum-seekers are being arbitrarily held in detention, in contravention of UNHCR Guidelines.[15] The Medical Foundation for the Care of Victims of Torture has documented cases where survivors of torture have been detained for prolonged periods. Amnesty International sees the extensive use of detention as an attempt by the previous government to deter potential asylum seekers. At the very least there should be time limits on the power to detain; detainees should be given the reason for their detention in writing; and effective monitoring and judicial safeguards should be put in place.

- The Asylum and Immigration Act 1996 removed the right to welfare benefits from two groups of asylum-seekers; people who claim asylum after arriving in the country and people appealing against a negative Home Office decision. This has caused severe hardship and suffering, leading Mr Justice Collins to declare in 1996:

I find it impossible to believe that Parliament intended that an asylum seeker, who was lawfully here and who could not lawfully be removed from the country, should be left destitute, starving and at risk of grave illness and even death.

- The 1996 Act also imposed an obligation on employers to check the legal status of their employees. At the time of writing, the Labour government has no plans to enact legislation to remove this burden from employers, although it is likely to lead to employment decisions being made on the basis of nationality and skin colour, thus legitimising and even encouraging racial discrimination.

Resource implications

Some of these four steps, like the ban on mines, would carry no additional cost to governments. Others, like the International Criminal Court, would carry a comparatively small cost when shared among the UN's members. Changing some economic policies to make them contribute to stability implies changing the priorities of existing spending from 'prestige' aid projects, for example, to basic health and education services.

In some cases, there is no way to improve the world's collective provision for stability and decent standards of relief without additional expenditure, or by forfeiting income, such as from arms sales. However, by the standards of the budget deficits and other demands on Western governments, the problem is small. Although regulation of arms exports might affect individual arms manufacturing companies, and employment opportunities in particular regions of producer countries, there is mounting evidence that there could, in fact, be a net *creation* of jobs if the huge subsidies currently given to arms exporters, in various forms, were used for investment in the civil economy.

Since 1993, there have been a series of suggestions for novel forms of international taxation to fund global priorities. Some of these ideas have shared the principle of 'green taxation' — that harmful things, like pollution, not good things, like wealth-creation, should be taxed.

One option, most famously suggested by Canada's James Tobin, would be to tax international currency speculation. A 0.25 per cent tax on foreign exchange transactions could provide around US$200 billion.[16]

What is still seriously under-funded, and could therefore benefit from these extra resources, are humanitarian and long-term aid, UN peace-keeping, but perhaps more importantly the local initiatives in the affected regions themselves, such as African governments' own preventive diplomacy and peace-keeping.

'Can do' diplomacy

The impression is sometimes given that governments are simply not interested in changing international policy in order to prevent wars and protect civilians. In fact there has been a determined effort on the part of some governments in the past few years to find the 'better way'.

The UN's new Secretary General, Kofi Annan, has shown an encouraging commitment to reform in some significant areas, but his success or failure will essentially be decided by the UN's member governments. Until now they have largely failed to provide the funds and diplomatic support to let the UN do its job well. This, probably much more than the UN bureaucracy's inefficiency and lack of accountability, has undermined the organisation's efforts. And the responsibility must fall most heavily on the five permanent members of the Security Council.

However, a number of governments, both from the West and the developing world, have effectively pressed for significant changes. The head of Oxfam International's Washington DC office, Justin Forsyth, discerns an interesting trend:

Ironically, it has been a number of less powerful nations who have led the way in trying to make the UN more effective. They have shown that political will combined with clear objectives can make a difference.

In terms of political leadership on the Security Council, it is often the non-permanent members who have led the way. It was New Zealand in 1994 who, despite US attempts to deny that genocide was taking place in Rwanda, pressed for a more substantial international response.

And it was Canada that consistently tried to show leadership in response to the deteriorating crisis in Zaire in October 1996.

The 24 governments who call themselves the 'friends of rapid reaction' — meaning supporters of a stronger stand-by UN military capacity — have developed realistic proposals, which have already begun to be implemented, to improve the ability of the UN to deploy troops quickly, including a mobile headquarters and a permanent army, with troops trained together, but stationed until needed in their home countries. The moves to see a total ban on anti-personnel mines by the year 2000 are similarly being pressed most vigorously by a group of governments, again led by Canada.

The Chilean UN ambassador Juan Somavia, and his Swedish counterpart, have been driving forces in pressing the Security Council to improve its information-gathering on wars from the humanitarian agencies on the ground.

A Better Way?

It is for governments and others to judge whether the steps suggested constitute the best way ahead. But there must surely be some way found to reduce the toll of civilian deaths in war which occur each year. As aid agencies, we have sometimes implied that the best thing individuals can do is give money to us to provide more aid. While funds for emergency and longer-term work are vital, Oxfam believes that an even more valuable contribution for individuals to make is to use their rights as citizens to tell their governments to find a better way of tackling the scourge of war.

Conclusion

The nature of war in the early twenty-first century could take two possible forms. The first is a brutal and bloody picture, showing continued killings of hundreds of thousands of civilians each year, tens of millions forced to flee their homes, still more facing unnecessary suffering. In this future, there will probably be more and more times when aid agencies refuse to play the 'fig leaf' to inaction by the international community (especially its wealthiest members), more times when the tough choice for aid agencies to make is to stay out. War's terrible images will be seen on television by the rest of the world in its comparative, and perhaps precarious, security. It will not feel like a 'global village' but like a world divided.

The other future is not a utopia. It is a dangerous and rapidly-changing world, in which many wars still go on, and many combatants choose to kill civilians in them. But there is more determined support for those people in countries trying to escape the vicious cycle of war, fragile 'peace', and war again; better targeted international policies to help to reduce the risks of future violence, and a more proactive international effort to protect civilians when wars break out. In parts of the world canvas, the picture is still brutal and bloody. But in other parts, this new approach is succeeding in preventing wars and enabling civilians to live in peace. Over the years, literally millions of people who might have died in armed conflict would survive to contribute to their societies. It is no longer the norm for the Geneva Conventions and humanitarian law to be flouted with impunity. People gain conviction that something can be done.

If the current trends described in the early chapters of this book continue, civil wars in the first years of the twenty-first century will produce even more human suffering, and aid will be still more compromised. The academic Mark Duffield wrote in his 1995 paper, *Symphony of the Damned*, that emergency aid now effectively has the prime purpose, for donor governments if not for generous individuals, of propping up an unjust economic world order. If those governments would challenge that charge as too cynical, they should use their power to make international economic policy directed more towards reducing poverty and less likely to fuel conflict.

It appears that governments do not do so because they do not perceive that they have to pay some of the costs of conflicts. Would rich world finance ministries which determine World Bank and IMF policies agree to stabilisation and adjustment programmes which accentuate poverty and social tension if the same ministries realised that they have to pick up the bill for humanitarian aid, and peace-keeping, when excessively austere programmes helped to push a country over the brink to war? Would they allow their foreign ministries a freer hand to, for example, negotiate at the Security Council for preventive deployments of peace-keepers, if they saw that the cost of peace-keeping might be a fraction of the cost of waiting for catastrophe and then being forced to pay for bigger operations? The UN troops in Macedonia, so far helping to keep the peace, have cost only US$134 million; a good investment when compared to a bill for more than US$8 billion for NATO's Implementation Force in Bosnia in 1996.

Similarly, would more companies develop codes of conduct to guide their business in vulnerable countries, if they perceived that their customers and shareholders expected them not only to protect the environment, but also to promote human rights and conflict-prevention?

One ground for hope is that there may now be a growing realisation that citizens, governments, and business have a long-term self-interest in peace around the world. It rests in part on the fact that, to some extent at least, Western governments cannot avoid picking up the cost of responding to civil wars, or at least those that are seen on TV. Their shocked electorates will not let them. Therefore they see the sense of investing in whatever makes wars less likely. Prevention *is* better than cure, though it is not always easy.

Though implementation will depend on the particular situation in each country, the principle which must run through all policies, is that every citizen should be encouraged to find a stake in peace. Fundamentally, peace rests on social responsibility. And this rests on people's belief that their interests are linked to, not opposed to, those of their society. Economic opportunities, the provision of services, and a commitment to justice, equity, and identity must combine to make this a reality.

Over the past few years this has been fundamentally threatened by the view that social cohesion and economic success are alternatives, not complements. This fallacy has lain behind much of the international economic policies which have helped to make many countries less stable.

This mood is now changing. The World Bank is gradually moving to see that economic reform can not succeed without a concern for human welfare. In a number of countries, including Britain, there has been a similar shift in the climate of ideas. As Tony Wright put it in March 1997:

A new language of public interest, community, stakeholding and security has already succeeded in puncturing the airy certainties of market individualism.[1]

If it has yet to be consistently applied to foreign policies, including international economic policies, it is hopefully only a matter of time. There is an urgent need for a new internationalist project, based on the value that human beings across the globe share a common humanity which gives people everywhere a responsibility to concern themselves with the suffering of others. This principle is embodied in the Geneva Conventions and all the international law that applies to war, which commits governments to help to protect civilians wherever they are threatened. In a very real sense, this gives people everywhere a stake in the foreign policy of all responsible governments. A 'stakeholding foreign policy' would not only look to a nation's short-term interests, but to the basic rights of all people.

Throughout, this book has tried to avoid oversimplifying the causes of wars, or being over-optimistic about the chances of solutions. Everything can not be done. But the 'something' which can be done, must be done. Nelson Mandela, speaking in Oxford in July 1997, observed:

Few would have imagined 50 years ago that the closing years of this century would see so much of humanity ... still blighted by insecurity stemming from violent conflict ... Few would have imagined that stability and security would continue to be under threat because so little has been done to reverse the growing gap between rich and poor.[2]

Reversing that gap, building that stability and security, should be the aim of an ethical foreign policy.

Notes

Introduction

1 Interview with Kay Willis of Oxfam's Resources Unit, February 1997.
2 This is the sum of figures for refugees and internally displaced people. Chapter 1 includes separate figures for these and deaths.
3 Kaplan, R (1996) *The Ends of the Earth: A Journey to the Frontiers of Anarchy*, New York: Vintage Books, p 436.
4 Smith, D (1997) *The State of War and Peace Atlas*, London: Penguin, p 42, table 14.
5 This average for recent years does not include exceptionally high years, such as 1994. Including Rwanda's genocide of that year would produce a very much higher, but perhaps unrealistic, average. Jongman, A J and Schmid, A P (1996): 'Contemporary armed conflicts', in *Prevention and Management of Conflicts*, Amsterdam: NCDO, pp 25–9
6 Oxfam believes that every person has a basic right to: a home, clean water, enough to eat, a safe environment, protection from violence, equal opportunity, a say in their future, an education, a livelihood, and healthcare.
7 US Committee for Refugees (USCR)(1997) *World Refugee Survey 1997*, Washington DC: Immigration and Refugee Service of America, tables 4 and 5. Figures accurate at 31 December 1996.
8 Bellamy, C (1996) *The State of the World's Children 1996*, Oxford: Oxford University Press (OUP), p 4.

Chapter 1

1 Interview with Mike Ash-Edwards of Oxfam's Campaigns Department, Tuzla, August 1995.
2 Red Cross figures quoted in Ignatieff, M (1997) 'Unarmed warriors', in *The New Yorker* 24 March 1997, p 64.

3 Jongman, A J and Schmid, A P (1996): 'Contemporary armed conflicts', in *Prevention and Management of Conflicts*, Amsterdam: NCDO, pp 25–9.

4 Bellamy, C (1996) *The State of the World's Children 1996*, Oxford: OUP, pp 10, 33.

5 Smith, D (1997) *The State of War and Peace Atlas*, London: Penguin, p 24, table 6.

6 UNHCR (1995) *The State of the World's Refugees*, Oxford: OUP, p 244

7 USCR (1997) *World Refugee Survey 1997*, Washington DC: Immigration and Refugee Services of America, Table 3 pp.4–5.

8 USCR (1996) *World Refugee Survey 1996*, Washington DC: Immigration and Refugee Services of America, p 10.

9 USCR (1997) op. cit., table 4.

10 USCR (1996) op. cit., tables 1 and 4.

11 Interview with Emma Gough of Oxfam's Resources Unit, March 1997.

12 Stojsavljevic, J (1995): 'Women, conflict and culture in former Yugoslavia', in *Gender and Development* 3:1 Oxford: Oxfam, p 38.

13 Camus-Jacques (1989), p 141, quoted in Crawley, H (ed.) (1997 forthcoming) *Refugee Women and the Asylum Determination Process*, p 3.

14 Beyani, C (1995): 'The needs of refugee women', in *Gender and Development* 3:2, p 29.

15 ibid, pp 29–30.

16 UNHCR (1995) *The State of the World's Refugees 1995*, Oxford: OUP.

17 Beyani, op. cit., p 35.

18 Despite all the coverage of Albania, Bosnia and Rwanda, this scale of the problem is far greater than most people in Britain realise. A MORI poll commissioned by the British Refugee Council and Oxfam in March 1997 found that only 23 per cent of those interviewed estimated that there were more than 15 million refugees in the world, only 13 per cent that there were more than 25 million. (Respondents were not aware of the legal distinction between refugees and displaced people.) Again perhaps surprisingly, only 29 per cent suggested that refugees were fleeing from war, whereas in fact most refugees are.

19 African and Latin American governments have agreed similar conventions which also limit refugee status to people who have fled their countries.

20 From report of visit to Angola, February 1997.

21 USCR (1997) op. cit., table 5.

22 International Federation of Red Cross and Red Crescent Societies (1997) *World Disasters Report 1997*, Oxford: OUP, p 135.

23 USCR (1997) op. cit., p.11, table 8.

24 Mussa Samizi, District Commissioner of Kasulu district, Tanzania, June 1997.

25 Letter to the author, September 1996.

26 Cranna, M (1994) *The True Cost of Conflict*, London: Earthscan.

27 United Nations Development Programme (UNDP)(1996) *Human Development Report 1996*, Oxford: OUP, p 149.

28 UNDP, ibid. Of countries that have not been at war for much of this period, fewer show a similar decline in per capita income.

29 Jongman and Schmid, op. cit, p 25. A more widely-quoted figure of 90 per cent is from Ahlstrom, C (1991) *Casualties of Conflict*, Uppsala University, Department of Peace and Conflict Research.

30 Watkins, K (1995) *The Oxfam Poverty Report*, Oxford: Oxfam, p 43.

31 Machel, G (1996) *The Impact of Armed Conflict on Children*, New York: UNICEF, p 1 of web site patterns.

32 Mackintosh, A (1996) 'International aid and the media' in Allen, T and Seaton, J (eds) *War, Ethnicity and the Media*, South Bank University.

33 Machel, G (1996) op. cit.

34 De Waal, A (1996): 'Contemporary warfare in Africa' in *Institute of Development Studies Bulletin* 27: 3.

35 *The Guardian* 26 March 1997, article by Gijs de Vries, leader of the Liberal and Democratic Group of MEPs.

36 El Bushra, J and Piza Lopez, E (1993) *Development in Conflict: The Gender Dimension*, Oxford: Oxfam/ACORD.

37 EU Investigative Commission into the treatment of Muslim women in the former Yugoslavia (1993): Final Report.

38 *The Psychological Well-Being of Refugee Children: Research, Practice and Policy Issues*, quoted in El Bushra, J and Piza Lopez, E (1993),op. cit., p63.

39 Stojsavljevic, J (1995) 'Women, conflict and culture in former Yugoslavia', in *Gender and Development* 3:1, Oxford: Oxfam, p 39.

40 Chinkin, C (1995) 'Violence against women', in *Gender and Development* 3:2, Oxford: Oxfam, p27.

41 Maxwell Stuart, L (1997) 'Domestic violence: old problems, new approaches', in 'Links', Oxfam's newsletter on gender, February 1997.

42 UNHCR (1995) op. cit.

43 Stojsavljevic, op. cit., p40.

44 Woodward, D (1996) 'The IMF, World Bank and Economic Policy in Rwanda', a paper produced for Oxfam, p2.

45 Deng, F (1995) 'Report on internally displace people'; report on Colombia produced by Francis Deng in his role as UN Special Rapporteur on Internally Displaced People, in October 1995, p2.

46 Interview with Kay Willis of Oxfam's Resources Unit, February 1997.

47 El-Bushra, J and Piza Lopez, E (1993), op. cit., p 31.

48 Machel, op. cit.

49 Bellamy, C, op. cit., p 19.

50 Figures from La Fundacion Social Colombiana, quoted in World Vision International (1996) *The Effects of Armed Conflict on Girls*, Monrovia, California: World Vision, pp 9–10.

51 Quoted in Bellamy, C, op. cit., p 14.

52 Children's Aid Direct (1996): 'Because of War', Reading: CAD.

53 Ahlstrom, C (1991) *Casualties of Conflict*, p 8, quoted in Bellamy, C, op. cit., p 13.

54 Machel, op. cit. p 1 of web site patterns.

55 Black, M (1996): 'Children in War', Reading: Children's Aid Direct, p 12.

56 The survey of 1505 children was conducted in June and July 1993 and quoted in Bellamy, C, op. cit., p 24; 55 per cent had been shot at, and 95 per cent had experienced nearby shelling.

57 Machel, op. cit, p 3 of web site summary.

58 ibid, pp 1-2 of web site psychology.

59 Suzanne Williams, Oxfam's adviser on gender and rights.

60 Machel, op. cit.

61 Bellamy, C, op. cit., p 18.

62 Machel, op. cit., p 2 of web site summary.

63 ibid, p 1 of web site patterns.

64 Goodwin-Gill, G and Cohen, I (1994) *The Role of Children in Armed Conflicts*, p 30.

65 Machel, op. cit, p 2 of web site summary.

66 *The Economist* 6 May 1995 'Sierra Leone: out of the bush', quoted in Bellamy, C, op. cit., p 18.

67 *The Psychological Well-Being of Refugee Children: Research, Practice and Policy Issues*, quoted in El Bushra, J and Piza Lopez, E (1993),op. cit. p 63.

68 Jongman and Schmid, op. cit. p.27.

Chapter 2

1 In legal terms, these rights are 'non-derogable'.

2 Twenty years later, many governments have still not ratified the 1977 Protocols.

3 Article 2, Universal Declaration of Human Rights.

4 Article 11, International Covenant on Economic, Social and Cultural Rights.

5   Quoted in Ignatieff, M (1997) 'Unarmed warriors' in *The New Yorker*, 2 March 1997, p.67.

6   In conversation with John Whitaker, Deputy Director of Oxfam (UK and Ireland).

7   Garcia, D (1995) 'Light Weapons and Internal Conflict in Columbia', paper presented to the American Academy of Arts and Sciences Conference, February 1995, Cambridge, Mass, p.13, Quoted in Louise, C (1995) *Social Impacts of Light Weapons Availability and Proliferation*, London and Geneva: International Alert and the UN Research Institute for Social Development pp.15–16.

8   Interview with Kay Willis of Oxfam's Resources Unit, February 1997.

9   Interview with Hasiba Harbash by Mike Ash-Edwards, Tuzla, August 1995.

10 Smith, D (1997) *The State of the War and Peace Atlas*, London: Penguin, p.9.

11 Macrae, J and Zwi, A (1994) 'Famine, complex emergencies and international policy in Africa' in Macrae and Zwi(eds) *War and Hunger*, London: Zed Books, p.14.

12 Jean, F (1995) *Populations in Danger*, Médecins Sans Frontières, London and Paris, p.15.

13 Sen, A and Drèze, J (1989) *Hunger and Public Action*, Oxford, OUP, pp. 274–5.

14 UNICEF 'Water, hygiene and sanitation'; internal training document, quoted in Bellamy, C, (1996) *The State of the World's Children 1996*, Oxford: OUP, p.23.

Chapter 3

1   Small arms are technically defined today as automatic weapons with calibers up to 20mm. Louise, C (1995) *Social Impacts of Light Weapons Availability and Proliferation*, London and Geneva: International Alert and the UN Research Institute for Social Development, p. 1.

2   Louise, ibid, p.10

3   Machel, G (1996) *The Impact of Armed Conflict on Children*, New York: UNICEF.

4   Smith, D (1994) *War, Peace and Third World Development*, New York: UNDP.

5   Much of this section is based on a study by Ian Woodmansey presented to Oxfam's Trustees on 29 March 1996.

6   Quoted by SaferWorld (1997) 'Humanitarian Aid or Band Aid?' promotional leaflet.

7   Louise, op. cit. p.7.

8   US Congress Research Service (199) *Conventional Arms Transfers to Developing Nations 1987-94*, Washington DC.

9   International Institute for Strategic Studies (1996) *The Military Balance 1996-7*, Oxford: OUP, p. 273.

10 Louise, op. cit. p.7

11 SaferWorld *Update* 18, Spring 1997.

12 Figures from the then UN Secretary-General, quoted in Randel, J and German, T (1996) *The Reality of Aid 1996*, London: Earthscan, p.xi.

13 IISS, op. cit, p.273.

14 Figures from SaferWorld.

15 US Congress Research Service, op. cit.

16 Human Rights Watch (1994) *Angola: The Arms Trade and Violations of the Laws of War*, New York.

17 UNDP (1996) *Human Development Report 1996*, Oxford: OUP, table 1.

18 US Congress Research Service, op. cit.

19 IISS, op. cit, p.273

20 ibid, p.283. Figures for China not available.

21 Cooper, N (1997) *How the UK Government Subsidises the Business of Death*, London: Campaign Against the Arms Trade, p. 4.

22 Eavis, P and Sprague, O (1997) *Does Britain Need to Sell Weapons?*, London: SaferWorld.

23 Press Conference, New York, 30 May 1997.

24 Smith, C *The Global Proliferation of Light Weapons*, London: King's College Centre for Defence Studies, quoted in SaferWorld, op. cit. p.3.

25 *Dawn* 25–30 June 1997.

26 Jongman, A J and Schmid, A P (1996): 'Contemporary armed conflicts', in *Prevention and Management of Conflicts*, Amsterdam: NCDO, p.27.

27 Louise, op. cit. p.6.

28 The incident took place in 1993. Garcia, D (1994) 'Light Weapons and Internal Conflict in Colombia', paper toAmerican Academy of Arts and Science Conference, February 1994, Cambridge, Mass, p.20, quoted in Louise, op. cit. p.13.

29 ibid. p.22

30 Louise, op. cit. p.15.

31 Wright, S 'New Technologies and internal security equipment; in the Proceedings of a Seminar on 'Stemming the Flow of Light Weapons and Security Equipment', May 1996.

32 Oxfam has supported mines-awareness campaigns and mine-clearance in a number of countries, and helped to provide artificial limbs and support for rehabilitation for mines victims.

33 Bellamy, C (1996) *The State of the World's Children 1996*, Oxford: OUP, p.26.

34 Machel, op. cit. p.1 of web site mines.

35 Figures from the Red Cross, quoted in Smith, D (1997): *The State of War and Peace Atlas*, London: Penguin, pp. 28–29, table 8.

36 For an account of the problem of landmines in Vietnam, see Monan, J (199) *Landmines and Underdevelopment: A Case Study of Quang Tri Province, Central Vietnam*, Hong Kong: Oxfam Hong Kong.

37 Interview with Kay Willis of Oxfam's Resources Unit, February 1997.

38 Smith, op. cit. p.28, table 8.

39 Interview with Dave Dalton of Oxfam's Resources Unit, February 1997.

40 Louise, op. cit., p.18.

41 Smith, op. cit., p.29, table 8.

42 ibid, p.28, table 8.

43 Louise, op.cit. p. 17.

44 Machel, op. cit. p.2 of web site mines

45 ibid.

46 Figures include sales to the Middle East, from SaferWorld (1997), 'Humanitarian Aid or Band Aid?', leaflet.

47 IISS, op. cit., p. 309.

48 Bellamy, op. cit. p.25.

49 Smith, op. cit. p.59, table 21.

50 Sen, A and Drèze, J (1989) *Hunger and Public Action*, Oxford: OUP, p.275.

51 UNDP, *Human Development Report 1997*, Oxford: OUP, Human Development Index Table pp. 146–7.

52 IISS op. cit. pp. 306–11.

53 Bellamy op. cit. p.14.

54 *Declaration and Programme of Action, UN World Summit for Social Development 1995*, chapter v, point 88 (c).

Chapter 4

1 Médecins sans Frontières (1993) *Life, Death and Aid*, London: MSF.

2 This comment was part of a contribution to the Florence Conference in June 1996 on 'The Role of Humanitarian Aid in Conflict Prevention' organised by the European Commission Humanitarian Office (ECHO) and Italian NGOs.

3 This was written in July 1997.

4 Joint Evaluation Follow-up Monitoring and Facilitation Network (1997) 'The Joint Evaluation of Emergency Assistance to Rwanda: A Review of Follow-up and Impact Fifteen Months after Publication', Copenhagen: JEFF.

5 ibid.

6 Jongman, A J and Schmid, A P (1996): 'Contemporary armed conflicts', in *Prevention and Management of Conflicts*, Amsterdam: NCDO., p. 27.

7 UNDP, *Human Development Report 1996*, Oxford: OUP.

8 Duffield, M (1996) 'The new humanitarian paradigm: from statutory obligations to relative values'; discussion document produced for the ECHO/VOICE Forum on 'Ethics and Humnitarian Aid', Dublin, December 1996.

9 In the 1990s, 20 countries, including Britain and the US, have achieved a higher per capita income rate than ever before. But average incomes fell by a fifth or more in 21 countries from 1990–93; and in 70 countries, average incomes in 1996 were below their level in 1980. Measured by the share of national income going to the lowest 40 per cent of households, Britain was the most unequal society of the top 20 industrial countries between 1981 and 1993. By the relative wealth of its top and lowest 20 per cent, it was the least equal bar one: Russia.

10 More than 23,000 people have died in South Africa's complex conflict; Jongman and Schmid, op. cit. p.27.

11 Smith, D (1997): *The State of War and Peace Atlas*, London: Penguin, p.86 table 33.

12 Randel, J and German, T (1996) *The Reality of Aid 1996*, London: Earthscan, p.xi.

13 Report from the US Mission to the UN, *Global Humanitarian Emergencies 1997*, New York, pp. 15–16

14 Randel and German, op. cit. p.13

15 Report from the US Mission to the UN, op. cit.p.16.

16 George Murray, Oxfam's Marketing Division.

17 Matthew Sherrington, Oxfam's Marketing Division.

18 Report from the US Mission to the UN, op. cit. pp. 15–16.

19 Figures from UN Department of Humanitarian Affairs, Geneva, June 1997.

20 Randel and German, op. cit. p.20.

21 There are, of course, exceptions. For examples of generous funding without huge media coverage, and for inadequate funding when there is massive publicity, cf IFRC (1997) *World Disasters Report 1997*, Oxford: OUP, p.56.

22 Much of this section is based on a speech delivered by Oxfam's Director, David Bryer, to the International Peace Academy seminar in Vienna in July 1996, further developed in an article by David Bryer and Edmund Cairns, 'For better? For worse?: humanitarian aid in conflict' to be published in late 1997 in *Development in Practice*, 7:4 Oxford: Oxfam.

23 Information from Nicholas Stockton, Oxfam's Emergencies Director.

24 USCR (1996) *World Refugee Survey 1996*, Washington DC: Immigration and Refugee Services of America.

25 Roberts, A *Humanitarian Action in War*, Oxford: OUP, p.79.

26 Oxfam decided not to provide dry food rations because these were more vulnerable to looting, despite the fact that the feeding programme would have been able to reach more people if it had done so. Not doing anything to encourage further violence against these civilians was judged as even more important than providing relief to the greatest number.

27 In fact, Toyota Land Cruisers are increasingly the mainstay of aid agencies around the world.

28 Bryer D, presentation to members of the UN Security Council, New York, 12 February 1997.

29 Brendan Gormley, Oxfam's Africa Director.

30 At one point, the Royal Air Force was quoting air cargo rates six times higher than one airline to transport the same relief to Rwandan refugees.

31 See Roberts, A (1996) op. cit. for information on recent increases in ICRC fatalities.

32 SCHR members include Oxfam International, the International Save the Children Alliance, CARE International, Caritas Internationalis, the Lutheran World Federation, the World Council of Churches, Médecins sans Frontières International and the International Federation of Red Cross and Red Crescent Societies (not ICRC).

33 UNHCR (1996) *State of the World's Refugees*, Oxford: OUP, p.37.

34 Mortimer, E (1996) 'The Future of Asylum in Europe', a paper delivered to the UNHCR Forum on 20 November 1996. The paper was based on one given at the 1996 Ditchley Conference on 'The Treatment of Refugees and Asylum Seekers'.

35 British Refugee Council (1997) *Statistical Analysis*, factsheet, p.1.

36 UNHCR, op. cit. table 11.

37 ibid table 9.

38 Mortimer, op. cit. p.3.

39 ibid. p. 5

40 Interview with *Berliner Zeitung*, quoted in *Time* magazine, 10 March 1997, pp. 23–4.

41 Huntington, S (1996) *The Clash of Civilisations and the Remaking of World Order*, New York: Simon and Schuster, p. 199.

42 British Refugee Council, op. cit. p. 3

43 Mortimer, op. cit.

44 Howarth, A (1997) 'In defence of the state' in *Fabian Review* 109: 1, Spring/Summer 1997, p. 12.

45 Interview with Anne-Marie Papatheofilou of Oxfam's Resources unit, April 1997.

46 Huntington, op. cit. pp. 201–2.

47 *Time* magazine, 10 March 1997, p. 22.

48 IFRC, op. cit., p. 17.

49 UNHCR,op. cit., p. 239.

50 Mortimer, op. cit. p.3.

51 Thomas Jefferson's policy of 'no foreign entanglements' is usually cited as the first example of US isolationism. Cf Clarke, J (1995) 'Rhetoric before reality' in *Foreign Affairs*, September/October 1995, pp. 2–7.

Chapter 5

1 Presentation to the seminar on 'Humanitarian Response and Preventing Deadly Conflict' organised by the Carnegie Commission on Preventing Deadly Conflict and UNHCR, Geneva, February 1997.

2 Randel, J and German, T (1996) *The Reality of Aid 1996*, London: Earthscan, p.ix.

3 Nicholas Stockton, Oxfam's Emergencies Director, in an internal Oxfam document assessing the situation in Burundi.

4 Halperin, M and Scheffer, D (1992) 'Self-determination in the New World Order', in Brown, M (ed) (1995) *The International Dimensions of Internal Conflict*, London: MIT Press.

5 Mackintosh, A (1996) 'International aid and the media' in Allen, T and Seaton, J (eds) *War, Ethnicity and the Media*, South Bank University.

6 Waller, D (1993, revised 1996) *Rwanda: Which Way Now?*, Oxford: Oxfam.

7 Brown, M (ed) (1995) *The International Dimensions of Internal Conflict*, London: MIT Press, p. 571

8 Atkinson, P (1996) 'The War Economy in Liberia' a study for Oxfam, SCF, LWS and CRS.

9 Stuart Sessions of Oxfam provided this comment, and information on Liberia and Sierra Leone.

10 De Waal, A (1996): 'Contemporary warfare in Africa' in *Institute of Development Studies Bulletin* 27: 3.

11 Interview with Sally Joss, Oxfam Campaigns Executive, June 1997.

12 Speech on 'Fifty years after Nuremburg' at Connecticut University, 15 October 1995, quoted in the International Crisis Group paper (1996) 'Aid and Accountability: Dayton Implementation', p.6.

13 Bell, R (1996) 'Truth commissions and war tribunals' in *Index on Censorship* 5/96, pp.148–50.

14 Johnson, C (1997 forthcoming) *Afghanistan: A Land in Shadow*, Oxford: Oxfam.

15 Nyerere, J (1996) 'Peace is the Product of Justice', address to the International Peace Academy, New York, 4 December 1996, p. 4.

16 Woodward, D (1996) 'The IMF, World Bank and Economic Policy in Rwanda' a paper produced for Oxfam, p. 3.

17 Maxwell Stuart, L (1997) 'Domestic violence: old problems, new approaches' in 'Links', Oxfam's newsletter on gender and development, February 1997.

18 Ignatieff, M (1997) 'Unarmed warriors' in *The New Yorker*, 2 March 1997.

19 Dasgupta, P (1992) 'Population, resources and poverty' in *Ambio* 21:1, pp. 95–101, quoted in Watkins, K (1995) *The Oxfam Poverty Report*, Oxford: Oxfam.

20 Summers, L (1993) 'The most influential investment' in People and Planet 12: 1, pp. 10-12, quoted in Watkins, K, op. cit.

21 *Time* magazine, 17 February 1997, p. 48.

22 Sen, A and Drèze, J (1989) *Hunger and Public Action*, Oxford: OUP.

23 ibid.

24 For a stronger criticism of the use of development aid, see IFRC (1997) *World Disasters Report 1997*, Oxford: OUP, p57

25 Brazil, for example, is a country with one of the most unequal distributions of wealth; which shows the limits of inequality as an indicator of conflict risk. The inhabitants of Rio's shanty towns have not, as yet, taken to armed conflict; perhaps this indicates the elasticity of the social fabric in Brazil. The 'Gini' the average for Africa (40). Vietnam (35) and Korea (34) are far more equal.

26 Levy and van Wijnbergen (1993) quoted in Watkins, K (1997) 'Globalisation and liberalisation', internal Oxfam document.

27 Figures from the International Monetary Fund/Economist Intelligence Unit (1996), quoted in Atkinson P (1996) 'The War Economy in Liberia' a study for Oxfam, SCF, LWS and CRS.

28 Atkinson, op. cit.

29 Interview with Kay Willis of Oxfam's Resources Unit, February 1997.

30 UNDP op. cit., table 1.

31 De Waal, A (1996) 'Contemporary warfare in Africa' in *Institute of Development Studies Bulletin* 27:3, p.9–11.

32 ibid, p.6.

33 With apologies to Clausewitz!

34 Atkinson, op. cit.

35 Keen, D (1997) 'War, crime and access to resources'; paper presented at a UNU/WIDER/Queen Elizabeth House meeting on 'The Political Economy of Humanitarian Emergencies',in Oxford, July 1997.

36 ibid.

37 In that year, the railway from the ore mine in Yekepa to the port of Buchanan was blown up. After that and other intense fighting in 1993–4, many foreign companies involved in the extraction of raw materials left the country, and those which remained have had to deal directly with the warlords, less and less formally.

38 Brown, M (1995) op. cit.

39 The warnings ignored are set out in Study 11 of the Joint Evaluation of Emergency Assistance to Rwanda.

40 Fitzgerald, V 'Global linkages, vulnerable eocnomies and the outbreak of conflict', paper presented to the UNU/WIDER/ Queen Elizabeth House meeting on 'The Political Economy of Humanitarian Emergencies', Oxford, July 1997.

41 Watkins, K (1997) 'Globalisation and liberalisation', internal Oxfam document.

42 UNDP (1996) *Human Development Report 1996*, Oxford: OUP,

43 Hanlon, J 'IMF pulls plug on Mozambique' in *The Guardian* 10 December 1996.

44 Watkins, K (1997) 'Worlds apart' in *Red Pepper* April 1997, p. 22.

45 Kaplan R (1996) *The Ends of the Earth: A Journey to the Frontiers of Anarchy*, New York: Vintage Books, p. 418

46 ibid p. 431

47 Stedman, J (1996) Negotiation and mediation in internal conflict' in Brown, M (1995) op. cit.

48 Bunting, I (1997) 'Hope is growing in the heart of Africa' in *The Journal* 12 April 1997, p. 10.

Chapter 6

1 Bunting, I (1997) 'Hope is growing in the heart of Africa' in *The Journal* 12 April 1997, p. 10.

2 Mandela, N (1994) 'African renaissance', speech to the meeting of OAU

Heads of State, 13 June 1994, quoted in *Granta* 48, autumn 1994, London: Penguin, p. 253–5.

3 Seybolt, T (1997) *Co-ordination in Rwanda*, Cambridge, Mass: Conflict Management Group, p. 45.

4 Overseas Development Administration (1996) 'Conflict Resolution and the Aid Programme', briefing for agencies, p. 6.

5 Drumtra, J in USCR (1996) *World Refugee Survey 1996*, Washington DC: Immigration and Refugee Services of America. p. 10.

6 Waller, D (1997) Presentation to the OECD Conference on 'Policies for the Prevention of Conflict', Paris, April 1997, p.1.

7 *Time* magazine, 7 April 1997, p. 17.

8 Oxfam (1996) 'Displacement in Colombia', Oxfam internal document.

9 Interview with Mario Balarine, head of the Council of Governors of the Chigorido indigenous communities, by Larry Boyd of Oxfam's Latin America Department, March 1997.

10 Oxfam's Latin America Department.

11 Interview with National Human Rights Monitors, April 1997, by Lukas Haynes of Oxfam's Africa department, who provided other information on Liberia.

12 Stojsavljevic, J (1995) 'Women, conflict and culture in former Yugoslavia' in *Gender and Development* 3:1, Oxford: Oxfam, p. 38.

13 Vesna Ciprus, Oxfam representative in Belgrade, and Sue Smith of Oxfam's Gender and Learning Team.

14 Kibreab, G 'The myth of dependency among camp refugees in Somalia, 1979-89' in *Journal of Refugee Studies* 6:4, quoted in UNHCR (1996) *State of the World's Refugees*, Oxford: OUP, p. 235.

15 Oxfam (1996) op. cit.

16 Interview with Dave Dalton of Oxfam's Resources Unit, February 1997.

17 UNHCR, op. cit. p.235.

18 Oxfam (1996) op. cit.

19 Interview with Dave Dalton of Oxfam's Resources Unit, February 1997.

20 The full name is Avega Agahozo.

21 Commission on Global Governance (1995) *Our Global Neighbourhood*, Oxford: OUP, pp 336–7.

Chapter 7

1 Roberts, A *Humanitarian Action in War*, Oxford: OUP, p.88.

2 Nyerere, J (1996) 'Peace is a Product of Justice', address to the

International Peace Academy, New York, 4 December 1996, p. 1.

3 Lecture given at the Holocaust Memorial Museum, adapted as an article in the *Washington Post* and *International Herald Tribune* 7 May 1997.

4 This figure covers the years 1900-80. Stedman, J (1996) 'Negotiation and mediation in internal conflict' in Brown, M (ed) (1995) *The International Dimensions of Internal Conflict*, London: MIT Press.

5 Figures from the Cambodian Red Cross, quoted in *Global Humanitarian Emergencies 1997* a report from the US Mission to the UN, New York, p. 9.

6 *The Guardian* 26 March 1997, article by Gijs de Vries, leader of the Liberal and Democratic Group of MEPs.

7 Charter of the United Nations (1945), p.1.

8 Labour Party (1996) *A Fresh Start for Britain: Labour's Strategy for Britain in the Modern World*, p.13.

9 Joint Evaluation of Emergency Assistance to Rwanda (1996) *The International Response to Conflict and Genocide*, Copenhagen: Steering Committee of the Joint Evaluation, p.47, finding A1a.

10 USCR (1996) *World Refugee Survey 1996*, Washington DC: Immigration and Refugee Services of America, p10

11 *Time* magazine 31 March 1997, p.14.

12 Somavia, J 'Ensuring the Security of People', Gilbert Murray Memorial Lecture, Oxford 26 June 1996, p. 19.

13 The President of the General Assembly, Malaysia's Razali Ismail, has suggested that there should be five new permanent and four new non-permanent members. The claims of Germany and Japan to permanent membership seem widely accepted. Less widely-accepted is how seats for states from Africa, Latin America and Asia should be chosen.

14 This is because some asylum-seekers fear that particular EU countries may have political links with their country of origin, which might prevent their application being impartially assessed. Existing regulations stipulate that application must be made to the country of 'first entry'.

15 Figure correct at the time of writing.

16 Watkins, K (1997) 'Worlds apart' in *Red Pepper* April 1997, p. 22.

Conclusion

1 Wright, T (1997) *Who Wins Dares*, London: Fabian Society, p.4

2 Mandela, N 'Renewal and renaissance: towards a new world order', lecture by President Nelson Mandela at the Oxford Centre for Islamic Studies, Oxford, 11 July 1997.

Other books in the Oxfam Insight series

The **Insight** series offers concise and accessible analysis of issues that are of current concern to the international community.

Rwanda: An Agenda for International Action
Guy Vassall-Adams
ISBN 0 85598 299 3, 72 pages, 1994

A Case for Reform:
Fifty Years of the IMF and World Bank
Oxfam Policy Department
ISBN 0 85598 301 9, 64 pages, 1994

NAFTA: Poverty and Free Trade in Mexico
Belinda Coote
ISBN 0 85598 302 7, 64 pages, 1995

Reforming World Trade:
The Social and Environmental Priorities
Caroline LeQuesne
ISBN 0 85598 346 9, 80 pages, 1996

Insight books offer concise and accessible analysis of issues that are of current concern to the international community and are produced by Oxfam UK and Ireland as part of its advocacy programme on behalf of poor communities. They are co-published with affiliates of Oxfam International. For more information about this book contact your national Oxfam.

Oxfam Canada
Suite 300
294 Albert Street
Ottawa, Ontario K1P 6E6
Canada
Tel: 1 613 237 5236
Fax: 1 613 237 0524
email: oxfam@web.net

Community Aid Abroad
Oxfam in Australia
156 George Street
Fitzroy
Melbourne
Victoria 3065
Australia
Tel: 61 3 9289 9444
Fax: 61 3 9419 5318
email: enquire@caa.org.au

Oxfam Hong Kong
9th Floor
Breakthrough centre
191 Woosung Street
Jordan
Kowloon
Hong Kong
Tel: 852 2520 2525
Fax: 852 2527 6307
email: info@oxfam.org.hk

Oxfam New Zealand
First Floor, La Gonda House
203 Karangahape Road
Auckland
New Zealand
Tel: 64 9 358 1480
Fax: 64 9 358 1481
email: oxfam@oxfam.org.nz

Novib
Mauritskade 9
2514 HD The Hague
The Netherlands
Tel: 31 70 342 1621
Fax: 31 70 361 4461
email: admin@novib.antenna.nl

Oxfam
United Kingdom and Ireland
274 Banbury Road
Oxford OX2 7DZ
United Kingdom
Tel: 44 1865 311311
Fax: 44 1865 312600
email: oxfam@oxfam.org.uk

Oxfam (UK and Ireland) publishes a wide range of books, manuals and resource materials for specialist, academic and general readers, and for schools. For free catalogues, please contact:

Oxfam Publishing
274 Banbury Road
Oxford
OX2 7DZ, UK.

fax: +44 (0) 1865 313925
e-mail: publish@oxfam.org.uk

We welcome readers' comments on any aspects of Oxfam publications. Please write to the editorial team at:

Oxfam Publications
274 Banbury Road
Oxford
OX2 7DZ, UK.

Printed in the USA
CPSIA information can be obtained
at www.ICGtesting.com
JSHW012040140824
68134JS00033B/3169